Virginia Fairweather

EXPRESSING STRUCTURE

THE TECHNOLOGY OF LARGE-SCALE BUILDINGS

Birkhäuser – Publishers for Architecture
Basel · Berlin · Boston

Layout and cover design: Anja Matzker, Berlin

A CIP catalogue record for this book is available from the Library
of Congress, Washington D.C., USA

Bibliographic information published by Die Deutsche Bibliothek
Die Deutsche Bibliothek lists this publication in the
Deutsche Nationalbibliografie; detailed bibliographic data is available in the
internet at < http://www.dnb.ddb.de >.

©2004 Birkhäuser – Publishers for Architecture, P.O.Box 133,
CH-4010 Basel, Switzerland
Part of Springer Science+Business Media
Printed on acid-free paper produced from chlorine-free pulp. TCF ∞
Printed in Germany
ISBN 3-7643-6666-4

www.birkhauser.ch

9 8 7 6 5 4 3 2 1

Contents

Expressed Structure and Building Technology in Design

An idea right for its time is a powerful force. In building design, at this point in history, three such ideas are expressed structure, collaboration and constructibility. In antiquity these aspects were naturally intertwined with building design. A successful project could only rise from the mind of a Master Builder who simultaneously considered function, structure and construction methods.

The Industrial Revolution brought an explosion of scientific knowledge, a flood of potentially useful construction tools, materials and methods, and a philosophy of labor specialization for greater efficiency. The resulting division between design and construction, and subdivisions within the design and construction fields, rendered Master Builders impractical for modern projects of any significant scale. A team of design and construction specialists could bring more cumulative knowledge to the table than any one individual. But divided responsibilities also brought divided philosophies and goals, setting the stage for less than optimal designs.

In recent years, more and more projects have been developed using the ideas of expressed structure, collaboration and constructibility to recapture the benefits of shared vision and intertwined knowledge. This book showcases a sampling of such projects through the work of Thornton-Tomasetti Engineers and highlights how all three elements were addressed through design and reflected in construction. This essay explores how everyone involved views the process and how collaboration contributes to a successful project.

What is "Expressed Structure?"

"Expressed Structure" describes a design with harmony between the structural system and the architectural form. The history of buildings helps define this somewhat abstract concept. Over centuries writers on building developed a vocabulary of architectural theory and criticism full of positive references to expressed structure: terms such as honesty, truth, directness, clarity and economy in design. It has long been applauded in architectural writing, with justifications that vary from beauty and appropriateness to a nearly puritanical moral rectitude. Generally "expressed structure" means a building design that is straightforward, logical and economical by following the dictates of the supporting frame. One can "see how the building stands" even if the frame itself is concealed.

Expressed structure can form a key aspect of building esthetics. Human beings respond intuitively to structural forms that "look right," much as they are touched by music with tonal combinations that "sound right." Expressed structure is pleasing to the eye and the intellect. There is an inherent appeal in the arch, for example, as a nearly ideal combination of esthetics and efficiency. In any building with expressed structure, the viewer can imagine the bare bones of the building, and how those elements behave in the the complete structural skeleton. Distilling a building down to its essence, its structural core, creates elegance and drama, a clear response to the demands of physics. Early Greek and Roman temples offer extreme, almost severe, examples of expressed structure. The columns and cross beams tell the entire story with majestic simplicity. The vaulted arches of later church architecture also express structure, as do the famous flying buttresses that surround the Notre Dame Cathedral in Paris.

Some more recent celebrated buildings have structural systems along or outside their skin in a manner reminiscent of those buttresses. Most designers are familiar with the Bank of China in Hong Kong, designed by I. M. Pei with structural engineer Leslie E. Robertson Associates. Visible steel X-bracing, wrapping the 1986 tower, resists typhoon winds on the prismatic, asymmetrical building. A monumental structural system is visible outside and within the atria of another Hong Kong example, Norman Foster's 1985 Hong Kong and Shanghai Bank, designed with structural engineer Ove

Arup & Partners. Foster has said that buildings must grow out of the "legible and fully expressed structure."

New York City's glass and steel Winter Garden by architect Cesar Pelli with Thornton-Tomasetti Engineers is an elegant exemplar of both expressed and exposed structure. The vaulted truss system is structurally rational, dramatic and almost totally open to view. The 1985 project was reconstructed after the September 11, 2001 attack on the World Trade Center. Both the original design and the modified but equally splendid current version are among the Thornton-Tomasetti firm's projects featured in this book.

Expressed structure is not always exposed structure, but exposed structure is always expressed. At the new New York Times Building by architects Renzo Piano and Fox & Fowle, structural detailing of the visible exterior supports received fine attention to express their function. At another New York building, the Times Square Tower by Skidmore, Owings & Merrill (SOM), huge X-bracing beneath its cladding is indicated on the exterior at only a few locations. The structural system is only partially expressed. Structural expression need not be obvious, notes Charles Thornton, Co-Chairman of The Thornton-Tomasetti Group. On the Petronas Towers by Cesar Pelli in Kuala Lumpur, Malaysia, one can "read" the structural system, with its cantilevers, columns and spaces, by looking at the exterior, he says, even though it is fully clad. Architectural theory and architectural criticism have favored different design approaches over the years. By the end of the 20th century and into the 21st, functionalism, and with it expressed structure, has connoted superior esthetics.

History

In U.S. architecture the underlying precept goes back to Chicago architect Louis Sullivan, whose major work was done in the late 19th century. His thinking became reduced to the catch phrase, "form follows function." Sullivan actually said "form ever follows function, and this is the law (...) the shape, form, outward expression, design or whatever we may choose, of the tall office building should in the very nature of things follow the function of the building." ("The Tall Office Building Artistically Considered," in *Lippincott's Magazine*, March 1896). Though widely used and paraphrased over the years, Sullivan's dictum is generally taken to mean that the interior program of a building dictates the outward form. The influence of Walter Gropius and Ludwig Mies van der Rohe, who embraced Sullivan's philosophy, is legendary in U.S. architecture. Earlier architectural focus on proportion and classical harmony has evolved to the "truthful" expression of structure, materials and function.

These ideas were embodied for years in the International Style, which has been defined as unadorned buildings that expressed structure through extensive use of exposed modern materials such as glass, steel and aluminum. The concept has persevered through other architectural "phases," modernism, post-modernism, or as critic Robert Hughes puts it, "messianic modernism," in which all ornament is eschewed. However, modernists did not necessarily expose the structure itself; often the cladding treatment was designed to hint at the structure which lay behind. A twist on this is a structure that is efficient, expressed, and even exposed, but conveys its contribution to the building design in a much more understated way. Richard Tomasetti, Co-Chairman of The Thornton-Tomasetti Group, describes the development of an expressed structure in Pittsburgh, Pennsylvania, by his firm for architects Welton Becket & Associates. Designed by David Beer, now with Brennan Beer Gorman Architects, One Mellon Bank Center has become a Pittsburgh icon. With glazing limited to address energy efficiency requirements and respond to an adjacent landmark stone-clad courthouse, the engineers proposed using the balance of the wall surface to structural advantage: an exposed steel façade that could serve as a principal wind-resisting structural element for the octagonal tower. The idea was irresistible to the steel-maker client. The resulting harmonious marriage of structural and architectural design takes full advantage of material properties. Window-pierced steel panels form a stressed skin tube that works much like an aircraft fuselage. This building's structure is exposed on the façade and indeed forms the expression of the building, but its structural nature is not obvious to the viewer.

The underlying theme of all these design approaches is economy and efficiency. For design purity, buildings should express the structural system and behavior, appropriate use of materials and construction practicality. Structure relates to esthetics through visual impressions of efficiency and lightness. Minimizing structural system weight and using less material to reduce overall weight and costs will, ideally, lead to an elegant building. In the 19th century, Chicago architect William Le Baron Jenney said designers should use "sufficient material and no more," a precept that holds true today. "Honoring the materials," in the words of 20th-century architect Louis I. Kahn, is an important part of the design process. Choosing the appropriate materials for the structural system and the optimum use of those materials is at the heart of design. Expressed structure is not merely a conceit based on honesty of purpose. Buildings with expressed structure can also function better and more economically.

Collaboration

Building an "irrational" design can cost a lot of money. Collaboration is the key to avoiding irrational design. At each step both architectural and engineering aspects must make sense on their own and within the overall building system. Advancing the design requires that all participants on the team be sensitive to the issues the others are considering.

Structural engineering students learn about columns, beams and connections, but learning to create the most efficient structural form within a design team is a high-er goal. When the architects and the engineers collaborate at the onset of design, the final result should look elegant and appealing, as well as correct. Some theorists make this distinction: a building's architectural expression emanates from overall form and cladding, while structural expression arises from the inherent form of the skeleton.

Structural designers look for an efficient structural system that eliminates the unnecessary. They seek to reduce the load-carrying members and to minimize component sizes and costs. Loads should be carried in the simplest and most logical manner possible within the architect's design. This effort also leads to a clear distinction between the structural members supporting the building and non-structural members addressing other design requirements.

Expressed structure relies on an important dialogue between the architect and the structural engineer. This interaction also benefits other parties to the design process, contractors among them. High-level collaboration early in the design process is becoming recognized as very beneficial, but it is by no means universal. Some architects want to work with the structural engineers from the start, so the design reflects structural needs naturally. Others, who prefer making individual statements and view outside suggestions as insults, say: "Here's my vision, build it." To be fair, the level of collaboration can also change depending on the nature of the project. Tall buildings and long-span halls quickly become impractically expensive if structural needs are not considered early. On the Petronas Towers in Kuala Lumpur, Cesar Pelli stated that the Towers could not have been built without the engineering design input of Charles Thornton; the firm's engineers "understand the architectural goals, and work to complement the design in the best way – they are brilliant engineers."

Smaller buildings can have more arbitrary designs and still be affordable. Even so, such projects will also benefit from early collaboration.

8

The successful integration of architecture and structural engineering requires a meshing of ideas and creative spirit between the designers. Architect Anne Haynes of Cesar Pelli & Associates worked with Thornton-Tomasetti Engineers on the Overture Center for the Arts in Madison, Wisconsin. In her view, the firm's engineers see each project as a design problem, not as a static issue; "they approach design just as architects do; there is a kinship in the aspects of shaping and expressing space."

Joseph Burns, a Managing Principal of Thornton-Tomasetti, is an engineer and an architect. He believes practitioners of both professions can learn from each other. The firm sometimes has the "good fortune" to work on projects where architects seek to share ideas with the engineers. For example, an opera house designed by Norman Foster for Dallas, Texas, is, at this writing, in the early stages of design-team meetings, that include Thornton-Tomasetti Engineers. On the most successful collaborative projects, designers see the structural frame-work as part of the order of the space they are designing, says Burns, and they want to know what the options are and how they might use them in the overall design.

According to another Managing Principal, Thomas Scarangello, the firm likes architects "who recognize the importance of sitting down early in the design stages, who enjoy the collegial process and welcome engineers with ideas." While anything can be built "if you throw enough steel and concrete at it," he thinks the engineer's early input can result in economy and good design. Most of what the firm does is unusual in some way, even unique. Some engineers are excited by complicated problems, and some seek the simple and elegant solution to what could have been complicated. Concerning for example the Gaylord Entertainment Center in Nashville, Tennessee, a design with highly complicated geometry, the structural engineers found subtle changes that made the design work better, and the architects, Hellmuth, Obata + Kassabaum, welcomed their design contribution.

The Engineer's Role

"The structural engineer's role is interpreting the archi-tecture; we are the bridge between the architect and the owner," says Leonard Joseph, Principal at Thornton-Tomasetti. He believes structural engineers should par-ticipate in the design process with enthusiasm, while keeping a critical eye on cost and constructibility. Engineers can and should offer alternatives so the ori-ginal design can be retained at the price the owner wants. For example, on the Lucent Technologies Buildings near Chicago, Illinois, Philip Kinsella of Kevin Roche John Dinkeloo and Associates notes that, "the structural system was consistent with the architecture, and Thornton-Tomasetti Engineers suggested solutions and alternative approaches that resulted in a more refined expression of goals." They respected con-structibility and durability.

For Robert DeScenza, Executive Vice President of The Thornton-Tomasetti Group, integrating architectural vision with structural engineering possibilities involves both conceptualization and practicality. Some engin-eers who "immediately grasp the theory of a structure, the architect's concept," can get to its essence at once. For the Philips Arena in Atlanta, Georgia, Bernardo Fort-Brescia of Arquitectonica noted the engineers' "sens-itivity to design issues." Architect Joseph Caprile of Lohan Caprile Goettsch Architects appreciated "the engineers' quest for creative solutions" on the Soldier Field complex in Chicago. For Managing Principal Aine Brazil, apprehending the architect's vision is important, but she extends the concept: engineers must have the skills to intuit what the client really wants and needs.

Such an engineer is invaluable to the design team, but it is also critical to include a talented, but highly practical engineer to flesh out the concept. That indi-vidual should also have excellent communication skills, especially with contractors. There is a parallel with architectural firms who have both design architects and working groups who apply the design.

In an ideal world, all projects would begin early design stage meetings with an exchange of ideas between the owner, the architect and the engineers. In the real world, construction cultures can affect how buildings are designed and built. Countries and cities often have an established network of designers and constructors who do things a certain way. Sometimes the design effort is focused on feasibility. If no cost-effective way to build can be found, the project will not be built. The dynamics can be very subtle as well as complex. Design team members frequently represent a contentious array of parties. Depending on the contractual arrangements, the engineer may be working for the architect, the owner or the contractor, which can complicate the process. The architect wants his or her vision brought to reality. The owner bearing the long-term financial risk wants to make a profit and attract potential buyers or renters. The contractor keeps one eye on schedule and the other on costs. Since everyone has a different stake in the project, give and take in the creative process can be hard work indeed. Some tension between the project parties is inevitable, and every participant on the design team must be consummately tactful or risk creating a minefield. Whatever the relationships are for the particular project and whatever the architect's vision, structural engineers have enormous responsibility for public safety. That reality underlies discussions of innovation in design or construction and of economic feasibility.

A recent *New York Times* article highlighted a change in the way that architects and engineers work together, and an increase in the engineers' contribution to the final designs. Some design professionals commented that "the younger the architect, the more likely he or she will want to sit down with the engineers and the client together." Prominent industry observer David Billington of Princeton University's engineering school said "engineers are revolutionizing design, creating new forms that technically and esthetically extend the boundaries of architecture."

The Economics of Design

The advent of design-build projects may have also accelerated this shift in the engineer's role. When contractual arrangements accord the engineers more risk and a greater stake in the project's success, it makes sense that they contribute to the end result. Contractors, too, are having their say, predicting construction contingencies and contributing ideas on costs and schedules. More and more parties are participating at the early stages of a project, and the design team has become more balanced. This multi-disciplinary input benefits the owner and the public. Mustafa Afadan, SOM project manager for the UBS Investment Bank project in Stamford, Connecticut, observes that the structural support "was an integral part of the architecture." The main goal for the designers "was to create a large column-free space with a strong esthetic statement that was economical to construct."

Economics can influence building design in a variety of ways. At the Erie on the Park building in Chicago, in response to local construction costs at the time of design, steel framing was selected rather than a more conventional concrete system. For a steel framework, the bracing system is the key to making a practical building. In the design that resulted, "the architecture is the expression of the structural system," says architect Timothy Hill of Lucien Lagrange Architects. Dramatic exterior chevrons both brace the building and provide the esthetics, an example of integrated design.

With commercial buildings, economics decide whether a structure is built at all and knowledgeable architects collaborate with engineers to provide efficient designs. Exterior bracing at Times Square Tower in New York incorporates both structural necessity and architectural space planning. According to architect Christopher Fogarty, then with SOM, "there is no excess; the building is rigorously designed."

The perspectives of investors, developers and owners are also important. Developer Robert E. Selsam of

Boston Properties understands the economic issues at work. In his view, the benefit comes from engineers who are problem-solvers, who embrace the business goals of their clients, and who engineer toward those goals. They work to "make the architecture possible, rather than to impose constraints on the architects' ideas."

Collaboration and constructibility can also relate to design effort. For the New York Times Building, structural steel details for the exposed framing were developed far more than for a typical building, according to Robert Willis, Vice President of Forest City Ratner, the co-owners and developers for the project. This reduces esthetic, engineering and cost surprises during construction.

The integration of architecture and engineering includes constructibility considerations. They are the nuts and bolts of the design process, and sometimes construction constraints can drive the structural design. The design collaboration increasingly includes the constructors. Thornton-Tomasetti believes in designing the structural system so it can be built in the most efficient and cost-effective way. Charles Thornton says there is no "Chinese wall" between engineers and the contractors. The firm listens hard to all the parties.

At one project requiring large quantities of steel, the firm worked with contractors and steel fabricators in a unique "partnership for steel," says Tommy Craig, Senior Vice President of the New York developer Hines. The innovative approach involved detailed design documents that enabled pre-qualified bidders to arrive at their optimum estimated prices. The results accelerated construction and saved money. Construction costs need to be considered in the preliminary design stages of all projects. Sometimes, the lowest-cost structural system might increase costs to other trades. Paradoxically, a more costly structural solution might save on building height that more than compensates through great savings in cladding and other material costs. Other times, eliminating a single beam in the early stages of design can save costs elsewhere during construction. On a more basic level, numerous projects have used a form of truss designed by Thornton-Tomasetti to be economically shipped and easily erected. The contractor or the construction manager can also contribute to the design team's preliminary ideas. At the Petronas Towers, for example, the structural design of the skybridge and the complex erection scheme required an intense joint effort between the engineers and the contractors.

Conclusion

To recapitulate, expressed structure could and should arise naturally from the collaboration between engineers and architects. These two parties are the leads in synthesizing form and structure and in exploring the logic of the space. But they are not the only parties. The old compartmentalized approach to design, with owners, contractors, developers, designers and urban planners following their own agendas, is changing to recapture some of the ancient Master Builder's integrated perspective. A wider and more multi-disciplined exchange of ideas can only be a good thing. Buildings with expressed structure, the subject of this book, result from constructive exchanges between the design professions. The free exchange of ideas enhances the creativity of all parties and results in economy of design and construction. When this happens, everyone benefits, including owners and the general public.

Richard Tomasetti sums up the firm's attitude: "The engineers seek the structural system that best contributes to the overall building. The structural system cannot be self-serving. What is most important is its contribution to the architecture, and the function and cost-effectiveness of the building as a whole."

A Model of Creative Engineering

The core philosophy of The Thornton-Tomasetti Group has survived decades of growth and change. While corporate culture is an abstract concept, its effect on a firm's approach to work, to clients, and to its own longevity is very real. Successful design firms have a culture that attracts and retains talented individuals who are both independent thinkers and team builders.

For one firm, the continuity of purpose began in the 1960's when two young engineers, Charles Thornton and Richard Tomasetti, joined 40-person Lev Zetlin Associates (LZA) in New York City. Lev Zetlin's approach to engineering design and to clients left an indelible impression on the pair, now the Co-Chairmen of the 400-person international engineering and design firm, The Thornton-Tomasetti Group, Inc., which evolved from Zetlin's firm. Lev's ideas carry on through its principals and staff.

Zetlin was a phenomenon, a maverick in the New York structural engineering world of the 1950's. Only six years after founding the company and with a small staff, he won contracts to design 14 pavilions at the 1964 New York World's Fair, a highly visible and prestigious venue. He advanced through personality and daring. "He had guts," says Richard Tomasetti. "He often offered clients an innovative design option he had not actually worked out, but he had supreme confidence that his staff would find the answers." And they did. He built a reputation for being on the leading edge. Charles Thornton says Zetlin convinced clients his firm was more creative than others, and "forced us to be like him." Never satisfied with one idea, he thought of "something better every day." Zetlin also gave young engineers huge responsibility for design and management.

This charismatic tutelage left its mark on Thornton and Tomasetti and became embedded in the firm's culture when the young engineers acquired the firm in 1977. Abraham Gutman, Jay Prasad, Daniel Cuoco and Joseph Zuliani joined as principals to expand management, create a multi-disciplinary corporate philosophy, and set the stage for future growth.

The firm has grown steadily, acquiring smaller, well-respected design firms in other locations since the early 1990's. The Thornton-Tomasetti Group now has ten offices across the United States and offices in Hong Kong and Shanghai. Three divisions focus attention on particular markets: LZA Associates provides complete building design services for specialized facilities with complex systems; LZA Technology performs multi-disciplinary building investigations, restoration design and disaster mitigation; and Thornton-Tomasetti Engineers offers structural engineering design for architecturally significant buildings, the subject of this book.

The firm maintains a culture that balances freedom to innovate with the responsibility inherent in structural design. To Robert DeScenza, Executive Vice President of The Thornton-Tomasetti Group, the staff helps "clients attain their dreams in an innovative and economical way. We offer the design that gets built." DeScenza is based in the firm's Chicago office, a highly successful acquisition by The Thornton-Tomasetti Group. Founded in 1956 by well-known Chicago engineer Eli Cohen, the 15-person firm acquired in 1993 has grown to an office of over 70 staffers.

DeScenza is part of a succession plan begun in the 1990's with the creation of Managing Principals. He and the other ten Managing Principals will determine the firm's culture and direction in decades to come. Their observations illustrate the principles and values of Co-Chairmen Thornton and Tomasetti, shaping the company's approach to structural engineering today.

Thornton-Tomasetti is an unusual example of successfully managed growth. The principals have worked at instilling the firm's history and style, and at maintaining consistency through great change. DeScenza says the firm has a good record of hiring and retaining talented people who want to work on top-of-the-line projects and keeping them motivated. Engineers stay because of the unusual freedom and responsibilities they are accorded. "No one is hidden away in a back room," says Daniel Cuoco, President and Managing Principal of The Thornton-Tomasetti Group. "Many firms have one or two highly visible principals, while this firm has many people with stature in the industry. Young engineers are encouraged to present conference papers, to participate in client design meetings, and to show initiative." Managing Principal Aine Brazil adds that the firm has no strict hierarchies. Project teams are formed by skills, not titles, so the firm looks for young people with excellent communication skills and enthusiasm in addition to technical expertise. Through lecturing at universities, speaking at conferences and serving on professional committees, the firm is well-known throughout the industry. Their principals communicate with the best and the brightest young engineers, and university professors often recommend their most talented graduates to Thornton-Tomasetti. When new hires join the staff, experienced engineers mentor them to foster creative, independent thought. On the business side, Thornton-Tomasetti Engineers is so well-known that most clients are aware of their abilities. Often, they are invited to join several different design teams competing for the same project.

The firm seeks a balanced mix of project types. "We like to do innovative work, but our engineers don't seek to complicate design," says Thomas Scarangello, Managing Principal. Leonard Joseph, a Principal of the firm, elaborates: "We don't want to accumulate renderings for unbuilt projects, but don't want to be cranking out the same designs either. We want to enjoy our work." Career satisfaction through challenge and accomplishment is a key to retaining talent.

Huge responsibility is implicit in structural design, and more so in innovative structural design. The more innovative the design, the more critical it is to review: to check calculations and think about everything that needs to be analyzed. The firm's engineers challenge themselves, and each other, to consider overlooked possibilities and unforeseen consequences. During in-house peer reviews, experienced staff not involved in a particular project probes the designers' thought processes.

Career growth is also important. Scarangello emphasized that principals stay engaged in projects, technical issues and staff development to provide high quality design services, but also address management issues in real estate, diversification, marketing, and the economy. Not every talented engineer wants to manage. The firm's size and diverse workload allows staff with a wide variety of skills and interests to be used effectively and valued for their contributions. Managing Principal Dennis Poon says the opportunity to work in The Thornton-Tomasetti Group's different divisions also offers a learning experience rarely found elsewhere and retains the firm's "great pool of knowledge." He adds that young engineers from around the world want to join the firm, and their differing cultural backgrounds enhance company creativity. The firm does interesting projects, "everyone is dedicated, and the atmosphere is one of harmony."

Client relationships are crucial, as in any service firm. As collaborators, the engineers go beyond the technical issues to anticipate and respect the needs of their clients. They try to put their ideas in the context of other's problems, to show how they can satisfy the client's desires. Client satisfaction is a constant goal, so the principals hire engineers with compatible values of honesty and directness.

Richard Tomasetti sums up the firm's unique mentality: "We encourage our staff to take the initiative, to be proactive. Our people have the tools and abilities to innovate, and the confidence to be daring, to reach out and push the state of the art, but we never forget cost and constructibility." Those attributes, actively nurtured and emphasized by Thornton and Tomasetti, have been passed on to the Managing Principals and staff. They are the legacy, and the future, of the firm.

Skyscrapers

Towers have been potent symbols since man began to build. They go back for millennia, and their purpose has evolved over the centuries from protection and worship to the everyday necessities of modern city life and commerce. The way they are built has also evolved. At the beginning of the 21st century, there are skyscrapers all over the world, and new technologies and materials allow engineers and architects to build in previously unimagined ways.

Most tall buildings depend on a basic system of columns and beams. Beyond that, there are endless choices to be made by the structural designer and the architect as they work together to create an efficient and economic building. In all building projects, engineers must consider wind and gravity loads, fire and, often, seismic codes when proposing a structural system. Both strength and behavior must be considered: strong towers can still be unacceptably limber and uncomfortable to occupy.

Tall buildings require extensive analyses of gravity loads, wind and seismic loads, consideration of uplift forces from building overturning effects, and dynamic building behavior. Starting with basic systems for lateral load resistance, such as braced cores, outriggers, tubular frames, braced tubes and bundled tubes, the designers consider the relationship of building height to width, core dimensions, treatment of corner columns and the location and spacing of other columns. The system selected influences the load path and member sizes, and vice versa. In a braced tube design, a massive column in each corner is connected by large diagonals to the other corners, concentrating the load at those points. In a framed system, closely spaced multiple smaller columns are connected by beams, distributing load over many elements. A braced core keeps the perimeter unencumbered, but its slenderness can result in excessive flexibility. Cores can be stiffened by the introduction of outriggers, but they obstruct open floors and are generally limited to mechanical floors. The interaction of building shape, fenestration, floor usage and construction methods available means that there is no single optimal design. Each project must be studied using its own unique mix of characteristics.

Sites present more constraints. The nature of soils supporting the foundations can affect building placement and permissible load paths and values. Crowded urban areas may present other restrictions. Extreme wind conditions make occupant comfort more difficult to achieve. Sometimes tuned mass dampers are used to control wind response. For tall buildings, column placement is another driver. Most owners want usable interior space unhampered as far as possible by columns, and the structural skeleton has to accommodate this demand, as well as the desire for windows.

Designers weigh the appropriate materials for the project, principally steel versus concrete, or a combination of the two, and determine which can be best used in the structural design. A steel frame is lighter than one of concrete, but its flexibility can make the building more subject to sway, a factor in tall-building design. The heavier concrete frame increases foundation loads but can be stiffer than steel, and with modern admixtures its properties can be enhanced. Availability, building usage and transportation factor into the design equation, too.

For tall buildings, there are benefits to stiff central-core structural systems and for perimeter support systems. A proper engineering analysis studies several systems using different materials. The goal is finding the combination that best accomplishes the architect's concept, meets the owner's needs and budget, and satisfies the technical requirements for the project's structural performance.

In the following section, we describe eight tall structures and the collaborative approaches used for their design. Each illustrates the challenge of bringing an idea on paper or a computer screen forward to result in an actual building. To find the optimal design requires both creativity and compromise by all members of the design team. The eight buildings illustrate the broad range of collaborative structural solutions developed for a single building type due to the variety of conditions and requirements that apply.

The Petronas Towers in Malaysia held the record of the tallest buildings in the world at the turn of this century. Regardless of subsequent record-breakers, these towers remain an extraordinary engineering accomplishment. Their structural system derives in part from the earlier unbuilt Miglin-Beitler Tower intended for the city of Chicago. The 1989 design by architect Cesar Pelli with Thornton-Tomasetti Engineers would have been 2,000 ft (609.6 m) tall. Several conceptual approaches to the Chicago project were refined and later incorporated in the Petronas Towers, where the same design firms were selected. The structural system for the towers includes an extremely stiff concrete core and a softer perimeter concrete frame, a more sophisticated version of the Miglin-Beitler Tower. High-strength concrete, proposed for the Chicago building, was used at Petronas, a first at the time in Southeast Asia.

The selection of appropriate structural materials is one key aspect of design. Suitable materials are available locally, or can be imported at a reasonable price. They are also familiar to local construction workers, and can be installed using locally available equipment. For main building elements in Malaysia, concrete filled these requirements better than steel, as the specialized fabrication shops and heavy-lift cranes needed to build and erect massive steel columns were not available. Concrete also brought more subtle advantages. Concrete stiffness can be increased by going to higher strength, while all strengths of steel have the same stiffness. Concrete has greater inherent damping than steel, reducing sway and thus improving occupant comfort in windy conditions. And connections of complex geometry can be built more easily in concrete than in steel, as reinforcing bars can lap within the concrete rather than connect directly as with steel.

For all these reasons, the effort to produce high-strength concrete was essential to making the Petronas Towers design practical. The design also incorporates steel framing where it makes sense: long-span beams support the typical office floors. These steel elements were light enough to lift with available cranes and simple enough to fabricate locally. More importantly, floors of steel beams and metal deck were fast to erect, keeping up with the concrete core and column work. Schedule, particularly the time to complete one floor, is another key aspect of skyscraper design.

The skybridge was another design feature affected by the particular conditions in a tall building. While bridges between buildings are not unusual, the large amount of sway that can occur at upper floors is an additional challenge. Each tower was anticipated to move as much as 1 ft (0.3 m) at the Skybridge level. The bridge allows for the space between towers to squeeze and stretch more than two feet, and also twists to accommodate towers moving at right angles to it. To keep the bridge centered and share expansion joint travel between both ends, an arch is used. Its erection method also had to allow for building motions while lifting huge assemblies more than 500 ft (152.4 m).

The Petronas Towers as well as the other projects in this section are successful examples for design team collaboration and special demands. In two buildings featured here, expressed diagonal bracing is a key architectural feature. At Chicago's Erie on the Park, a 24-floor residential tower, the engineering and the architecture are virtually inseparable. The structure is expressed in bold exterior bracing. The design resulted from the collaboration of architect Lucien Lagrange and the engineers in solving the problems posed by the narrow irregular site, the consequently irregular building shape, and the need for floor space that allows for apartments of varied sizes. This project also demonstrates how high-tech computer capabilities can enhance structural design and facilitate construction. Thornton-Tomasetti

Engineers created a 3-D Xsteel model that allows system geometry and member dimensions to be exported to the steel fabricator, simplifying the process and reducing errors in construction.

At the new Times Square Tower in the heart of Manhattan, a severely restricted site resulted in the selection of a perimeter-braced tube system. Each face of the slender tower is stiffened by vertical cross-bracing from corner to corner. Architect SOM and Thornton-Tomasetti Engineers found the X-bracing to be the optimum solution to enhancing rentable space in an exceedingly narrow trapezoidal footprint. While giant X-braced modules occur on all the building faces, they are only hinted at on the patterned and colored glass cladding. On one side, a zigzag design down the façade replicates half of the large X's beneath the tower's skin, a touch of drama appropriate for its location above brash Times Square. Tying the 49-story building's structural system to the maze of subway tunnels below grade was another collaborative engineering accomplishment.

Existing building foundations, initially considered an obstacle at the Bank One Corporate Center in Chicago, became part of a unique solution. Thornton-Tomasetti Engineers devised a method to transfer gravity loads from a modern building grid to allow the re-use of a foundation placed before the 20th century on a very different grid. The design solution made the downtown site economically feasible. Above ground, a sloped column system allowed the building to project over the public right-of-way, adding column-free floor space. This steel transfer system involved massive connections, but proved more economical than other approaches explored by the engineers and the architects, DeStefano & Partners and Ricardo Bofill.

The optimum use of building materials is a constant design goal. At New York City's new 50-floor Random House tower, architect SOM used concrete and steel to differentiate the residential floors from the publisher's office floors. The apartment levels have an all-glass curtain wall, while the office areas are clad in stone and steel. Inside, the engineers developed a steel structural frame for the lower 25 floors, and a concrete structural frame above. An intricate but cost-effective transfer system between the two building materials employs steel girders and a series of trusses that act both as gravity transfer elements and as lateral load outriggers. A pair of liquid column dampers reduce wind sway for occupant comfort.

At another tall building, China's Plaza 66, the designers explored a variety of construction materials and structural systems to achieve the owner's goals. The client wanted a tall, slender building at a windy site with poor subgrade soils. There were stiffness issues for this 963 ft (293.5 m) high tower due to its narrow footprint. Architect Kohn Pederson Fox and Thornton-Tomasetti worked with local code officials to reinterpret overly conservative wind sway provisions, and the resulting waiver made the project economics feasible. The engineers developed several structural systems for the tower; the concrete core-and-outrigger solution proved far less costly than those using other schemes due to locally available materials, labor and equipment. Outriggers occur on mechanical floors. A cellular concrete mat helped overcome the foundation difficulties. At the tower's top, steel was the material of choice because of its light weight. A steel visor cantilevers out from the building below a ten-story glass lantern with a steel frame.

In New York City, Thornton-Tomasetti worked with architects Renzo Piano and Fox & Fowle on the new New York Times Building. Piano's concept is a vivid example of expressed structure. Within the building is a steel-braced core with outriggers. For additional stiffness against sway, another set of large-scale steel X-braces is exposed on its exterior. Steel is economical to purchase, fabricate and erect in New York City. An additional benefit for this project is the slender appearance of steel: the steel framing is backed by glass that works with off-white ceramic screens to create the illusion of lightness. Concrete would provide a very different visual impression. There is little that is purely ornamental in the design of this building's framing. The structural system is the architecture.

These towers all illustrate the best use of material properties and problem-solving to address project-specific challenges, including expressed and exposed structures where the structural engineering design creates visible architecture.

Petronas Towers, Kuala Lumpur

At 1,483 ft (452 m), the Petronas Towers in Kuala Lumpur, Malaysia, were the tallest buildings in the world at the end of the 20th century. That statistic guaranteed global attention, but beyond the daring height lies a story of design collaboration.

The project began with an architectural competition that called for a "uniquely Malaysian" building, the gateway to a city center. While the design requirements were sparsely defined, the winning concept emphasized geometric shapes widely used in Muslim structures. The jury chose the slender, tapering twin towers and Islamic-inspired, star-shaped floor plans of architect Cesar Pelli of New Haven, Connecticut (Fig.1). The eight-pointed star, a dominant motif in Muslim art, was formed by superimposing two squares rotated by 45 degrees (Fig.2).

1 Tapering twin towers created a building group with a unique and immediately identifiable profile for Malaysia.

Bringing this conceptual design to reality required give-and-take between architect and engineer. Pelli comments on the process, saying "Thornton-Tomasetti Engineers are good collaborators and brilliant engineers – they understand the architect's goals and work to complement the architecture in the best possible way."

That process required studies of materials and systems. For materials, Petronas Towers' structural system emphasized concrete familiar to local contractors, readily available and less costly than steel. Concrete also has mass, stiffness and damping properties appropriate for an 88-story structure subject to windy conditions. The engineers took the material up a notch by introducing high-strength concrete to Southeast Asia, incorporating additives such as silica fume and superplastizers. Concrete used for Petronas Towers has 10,000 psi concrete strength by U.S.-style cylinder tests (80 MPa by European-style Cube tests) and 25% better stiffness than the 6,250 psi (50 MPa) concrete previously used in Malaysia and often used in the United States. The stronger, stiffer material allows members to be smaller and lighter, an advantage in very tall buildings. Thinner columns left more floor space. Cast-in-place elements could be placed efficiently without heavy rigging, and complex joints with awkward geometry could be constructed using simple methods.

For systems, the engineers began by studying perimeter "tubular frames," casting the wall as an extrusion with punched windows. Picture a chimney with an intricate fluted plan. Then imagine window openings cut through the side of each flute, leaving a "column" of solid wall at each corner fold. This approach offered economy and vast views, but lacked sufficient stiffness. The final floor plan of points and arcs would have twenty-four 90-degree turns and eight 135-degree curves, softening perimeter frame behavior. Another approach, cutting windows at "folds" and leaving columns at the mid-face of each flute, could minimize the softening effect of turns but would substantially intrude into views (Fig.3).

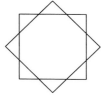

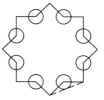

2 Tower floor plans were developed in five steps.
From top to bottom:

The basic square.

Two interlocking squares rotated 45 degrees form a classic Islamic pattern.

The outline is an eight-pointed star.

Circular arcs, inserted for more usable floor space, stay behind the dashed line to keep the profile sharp.

The resulting 16-branched form.

3 Half-plans show early structural concepts studied for a concrete perimeter tube frame:
Top: window openings occur between corners. Under wind loads, the L-shaped corner columns would experience biaxial bending and reduce frame stiffness.

Bottom: columns occur mid-face and windows wrap around corners. Biaxial column bending and loss of frame stiffness is avoided but columns would block views.

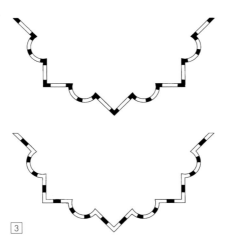

The innovative support system finally developed combines an extremely stiff concrete core and a softer perimeter concrete frame with columns only at interior corners (Fig.4). Views are open. The system supports vertical loads and resists wind loads from the mild Malaysian climate; earthquakes and typhoons were not a significant design concern. The perimeter columns vary in diameter and concrete strength as they rise upward and step back to create the tapered tower tops (Fig.6).

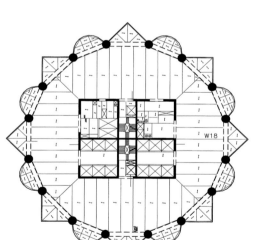

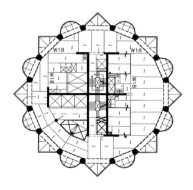

4

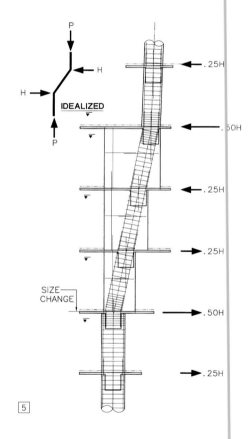

5

4 The lower half of the Petronas Towers have a "bustle," or smaller connected floor area, in addition to the main tower. Note these key elements:
A Twelve concrete columns surround the bustle; 16 columns surround the tower.
B Steel beams support floor slabs, typically with 4.3 inch (110 mm) deep concrete fill including 2 inch (53 mm) metal deck. W 18 indicates I-beam, 18 inch deep (equivalent metric size: UB 460).
C Concrete beams link the columns to form ring frames around the tower and bustle.
D Bands of steel reinforcing bars tie the bustle back to the tower core.
E The core is a box of concrete shear walls. Express elevators run to levels 41/42.

5 To provide setbacks without transfer girders, columns are sloped inward over three stories and reinforcing bars are added to ring beams and floor slabs to resist the lateral thrusts.

To work with double-deck elevators, all floor-to-floor heights had to be 13.1 ft (4 m). This prohibited deep transfer girders at the setback levels. The engineers' solution was to slope the columns inward below each setback floor, eliminating the need for transfers (Fig.5).

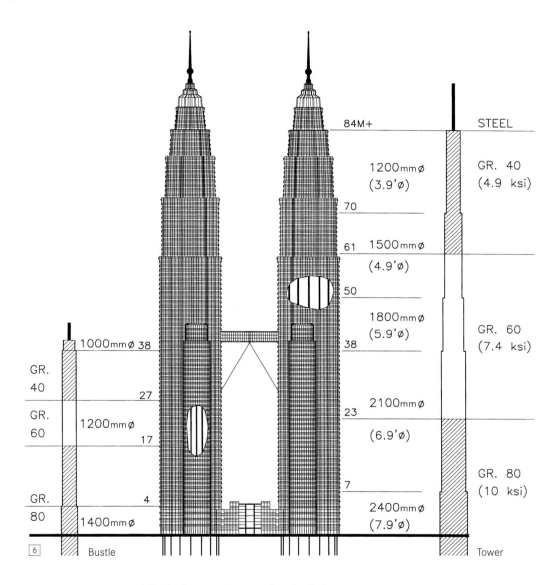

6 Cast-in-place concrete core walls and perimeter columns and beams use eight sizes and three concrete mixes, from 4,900 psi to 10,000 psi (40-80 MPa), to optimize size, strength, stiffness and cost. Steel columns are at the tops of towers and bustles.

Concrete ring beams link the columns to form the lateral load-resisting perimeter frame. The beams are haunched (Fig.8,9) to accommodate mechanical systems in the ceiling plenum. Concrete outriggers between the 38th and 40th floors connect the core to the perimeter columns, increasing stiffness and resistance to lateral loads.

The use of core walls and perimeter frames made the floor plan exceptionally open, providing the owners with ample usable space, almost 75% of the gross area. The wide spacing of perimeter columns also affords grand views and further enhances the rental space. On the towers' exteriors, stainless steel features shade sunlight and shed water (Fig.13). The self-cleaning shades also add visual interest through increased surface texture and reflection of sunlight at different angles than the tower skins.

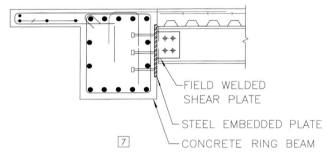

FIELD WELDED SHEAR PLATE

STEEL EMBEDDED PLATE

7

CONCRETE RING BEAM

7 To speed construction, concrete beams and walls had flush steel plates cast in; the steel erector later field-welded shear connection plates to them in precise locations for subsequent bolting to steel beams.

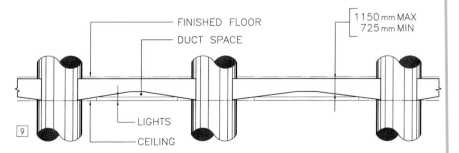

FINISHED FLOOR

DUCT SPACE

1150 mm MAX
725 mm MIN

LIGHTS

9

CEILING

8 The haunched or "bow tie" concrete ring beams were clearly visible during construction.

9 Concrete ring beams are haunched, or tapered in a bow tie shape in elevation, to maximize moment frame stiffness against wind while allowing air ducts and ceiling lights to pass below.

Although concrete is the most prevalent construction material in the area, the engineers incorporated steel in the structural system where construction efficiency outweighed material cost. Between the concrete core and ring beams, steel wide-flange beams provide long spans and fast erection. Swift construction was a priority for this project. Contractors used core wall forms that climbed on their own jacks (Fig.11). To keep up, erection crews fastened steel beams to steel plates embedded on the sides of core walls and concrete ring beams (Fig.7). Metal deck was then spread on the beams, and floor concrete was placed on the deck without slowing core and column work. Points and arcs are steel-framed cantilevers (Fig.10). The top four floors are relatively small due to building taper, so narrower steel columns and ring beams were used instead of concrete. Steel also frames the pinnacles that top off the towers (Fig.14).

10 Several floors below the concrete construction activity, cantilevered steel trusses are installed to carry the distinctive points and arcs of the Petronas Towers' design.

11 This crane-bucket view shows that the concrete core and concrete perimeter columns and ring beams are advancing ahead of the floor framing.

23

The pinnacles punctuate the Kuala Lumpur skyline and are accentuated by lighting. Tapering bases of conventional steel trusswork clad with stainless steel panels support 216 ft (66 m) tall stainless steel masts. To guard against wind-induced vibration, a simple chain damping system is mounted within each mast (Fig.12). Petronas Towers, glimmering in their linen-finish stainless steel cladding, opened in 1999 (Fig.15). The project is part of a larger development complex, Kuala Lumpur City Centre, owned by KLCC (Holdings). Petronas, the Malaysian gas utility, occupies one tower. The title of being the world's tallest building may be eclipsed by other projects under construction, but the structural design of Petronas Towers will continue to be a landmark.

S.S.RUNGS @ 240 o.c.

200mm

S.S. VENTED HATCH AND CABLE

S.S.CROSS BAR

7600mm (25 FT)

400ø x 12mm S.S. PIPE

50 mm CLR

NEOPRENE SLEEVE OVER CHAIN

GALV. CHAIN 54 kg/m (36 plf)

FIN PROJECTS 15 mm (TYP)

12 MAST DAMPER

13

12 A rubber-sheathed heavy galvanized ship anchor chain freely swinging within a steel pipe acts as an inexpensive but effective damper, absorbing energy whenever the mast sways in the wind.

13 This close-up of typical façade panels shows lines of round and teardrop-shaped sun shades that encircle the building.

14 Erecting the stainless steel pinnacle mast required ingenuity. The sequence, from left to right:
Holes left in four floors created a safely enclosed vertical work space.
- Small segments were hoisted to a landing, then shifted to the work space.
- Segments from mid-mast to tip were erected first.
- The "ring ball" of curved stainless steel pipes was "parked" above.

- The mast's upper half was lifted part way by jacked cables or rods.
- Lower mast half assembly proceeded from base to mid-point.
- Mast halves were joined before jacks lifted them to their final position.
- Jacking paused to permit connecting to the ring ball.
- With mast in final position, floor holes were filled and pinnacle cladding was installed.

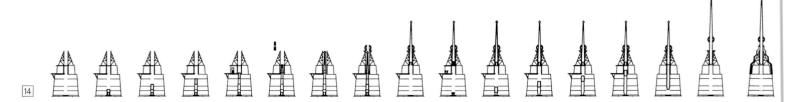

14

Owner
**KLCC (Holdings) Sdn. Bhd.,
Kuala Lumpur, Malaysia**

Developer
Kuala Lumpur City Centre Berhad, Malaysia

DESIGN CONSULTANT TEAM
Project Management Consultant
Lehrer McGovern International, Malaysia
Design Consultant
Cesar Pelli & Associates, Inc.
Technical Consultant
Adamson Associates
Structural Consultant
Thornton-Tomasetti Engineers
Mechanical & Electrical Consultant
Flack + Kurtz
Geotechnical Consultant
STS Consultants
Wind Consultant
**Rowan Williams Davies & Irwin,
Guelph**
Fire Safety Consultant
Rolf Jensen & Associates
Lighting Consultant
HM Brandston & Partners
Acoustic Consultants
**Shen Milsom & Wilkie – Towers
L. Kirkegaard – Concert Hall**
Elevator Consultant
Katz Drago & Co.

DESIGNERS OF RECORD
Architect of Record
**Architectural Division KLCC Bhd., Kuala
Lumpur, Malaysia**
Structural Engineer
**Ranhill Bersekutu Sdn. Bhd., Kuala Lumpur,
Malaysia**
Mechanical, Electrical & Plumbing Engineer
KTA Tenaga Sdn. Bhd., Malaysia
Geotechnical Engineer
Ranhill Bersekutu Sdn. Bhd., Malaysia

TOWER 1 CONTRACTOR
Mayjaus Joint Venture
**MMC Engineering & Construction, Malaysia
Ho Hup Construction Company Berhad,
Malaysia
Hazama Corp.
J. A. Jones Construction Co.
Mitsubishi Corp.**

TOWER 2 CONTRACTOR
SKJ Joint Venture
**Samsung Engineering & Construction
Kuk Dong Engineering & Construction
Syarikat Jasatera Sdn. Bhd., Malaysia**

SKYBRIDGE
Fabrication
Samsung Heavy Industries
Erection
VSL Heavy Lifting

CENTRE COURT STEEL
Victor Buyck

CONCERT HALL FIT-OUT
Comtrac – CCG Joint Venture

15 Stainless steel in linen-finish façade panels and brushed finish sunshades make the completed Petronas Towers sparkle in the sun.

Skybridge at Petronas Towers

A unique skybridge connects the towers, providing a link that both stimulates the imagination and serves as a symbolic gateway (Fig.1). The skybridge's sloping legs draw the eye upward, accentuating the space between the towers as well as their height. Beyond the visual enhancement, the two-story steel walkway offers practical advantages. It is fire-resistant and designed to function as a building exit in emergencies; the cost of the skybridge was largely offset by eliminating the need for an additional fire stair in the towers. The bridge provides circulation between the towers without having to descend to the ground floor and acts as a "Main Street" for nearby floors where shared facilities such as meeting rooms, a prayer room and an executive dining room are located.

1 The skybridge linking twin Petronas Towers creates a symbolic gateway.

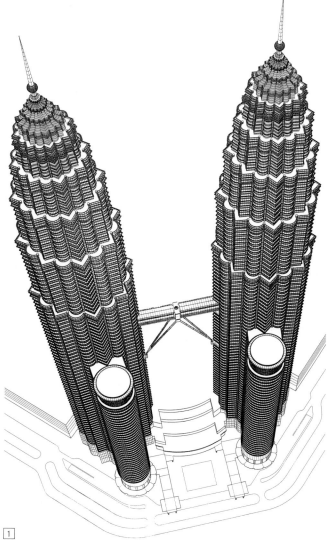

1

The engineers chose steel for the highly complex bridge because of the material's flexibility and ease of erection compared to concrete. They chose a shallow girder system for the walkway, supported at midspan by a two-hinged arch (Fig.3). This resulted in a more transparent bridge than a conventional truss solution (Fig.2). The components, almost 500 pieces in all, were shipped from South Korea, and structural elements were designed in lengths that simplified the shipping. For example, each leg has five segments that were field bolted in the on-site assembly.

Wind forces on the bridge and on the adjacent towers were important design considerations. For cross-wind, along-wind, and torsional forces on the towers, they could each move up to 1 ft (300 mm) at bridge level. To handle that movement, skybridge ends allow for up to 16 inches (400 mm) of travel in and out. The supporting two-hinged arch, with legs comprised of pairs of steel pipes 164 ft (50 m) long and 3.6 ft (1.1 m) in diameter, keeps the walkway centered and equalizes the bridge-to-tower joint movements (Fig.5). The design results in more acceptable joint travel. For tower movement at right angles to the bridge, the walkway has a rotational pin at each tower end and at the bridge midspan where it meets the arch crown (Figs.4,6).

2 Putting support structure below the floor allows for open, glassy walkway spaces.

3 Bridge walkways on levels 41 and 42 and roof are carried by a two-span continuous plate girder propped by pipe legs midway between the towers.

4 Girder ends move in and out of the towers freely, but are restrained against crosswise motion by guide pins. Legs can move on pivot bearings.

5 Steel pipe arch legs 43.3 inches (1,100 mm) in diameter meet at a pentagonal crossbeam to support continuous bridge girders. Each leg contains three compact tuned mass dampers at mid-height to control crosswind oscillations.

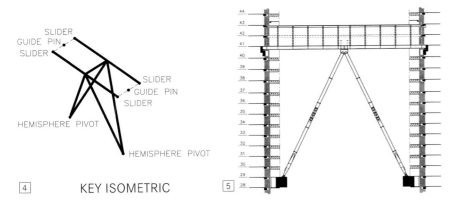

KEY ISOMETRIC

Each arch leg springs from a single spherical bearing on the towers' 29th floor (Figs.7,8). This allows for rotation in all axes as towers move. The legs rise at a 63-degree slope to the 41st floor where they meet at a crown cross-girder just below the two-span continuous girders that form the floor of the 190 ft (58 m) long skybridge (Fig.6). The upper walkway is at level 42 and the walkway roof at level 43. If the towers move towards each other the arch crown will rise, up to 4 inches (100 mm), but girder flex and curtain wall movements have been designed for that behavior. The engineers studied alternative structural systems such as suspension cables from above, but that would have doubled the amount of vertical travel, so the arch was preferable.

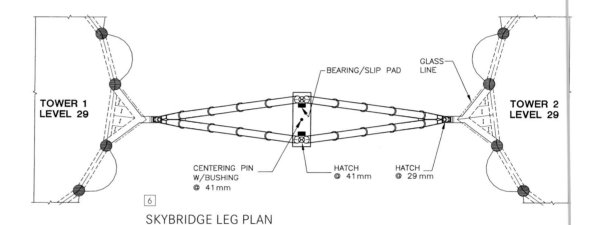

SKYBRIDGE LEG PLAN

6 Bridge arch legs meet above the Level 29 bearings to allow the bridge and towers to twist differently. Hatches at each end permit maintenance access throughout the legs and crossbeam. Bridge girders can slide and rock on slip pads but maintain their position by the centering pin.

7 Each skybridge leg pair lands on a Teflon-lined socket that glides over a polished stainless-steel hemisphere. The bearing allows for small in-out, left-right and twisting movements. It also permitted legs to tilt during erection. The U-bolt provided erection-stage security.

A more localized wind concern was leg vibration in moderate breezes. Wind tunnel testing confirmed the designers' expectations that such behavior was possible, due to low damping in the steel legs. To resolve it, the engineers placed three tuned mass dampers in each sloping leg between the 34th and 35th floors. These twelve dampers reduce wind-excited leg vibrations, mitigating movements and avoiding metal fatigue. Self-weight bending stress in the legs was another design consideration; the engineers built in camber, incorporating a slight upward/outward curve of 16 inches (400 mm) at mid-height of each leg. This camber uses axial load from bridge weight to offset potential bending, and counteracts the illusion that straight legs curve inward.

8 Creating economical, accurate forks of large diameter pipe required strategic detailing. Upper pipes are cut to a bevel and reinforced with a central plate.
At mid-height they transition to a "racetrack" section of half-pipes and flat plates. Just above the hemispherical bearing, a true cone short enough for accurate brake bending is used. The leg hatch is a custom design with counterweights and baffled vents.

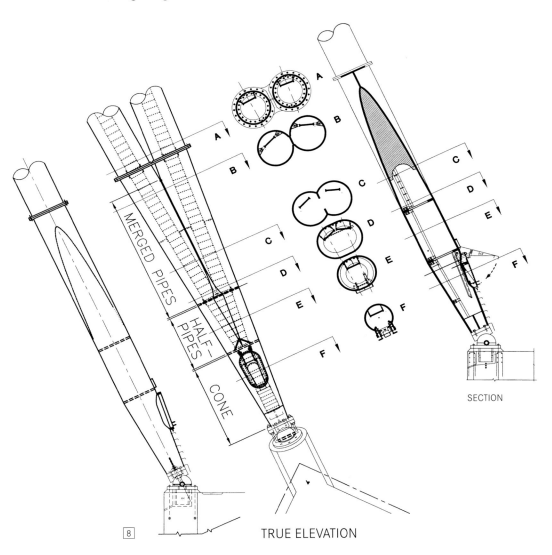

MERGED PIPES

HALF-PIPES

CONE

8

TRUE ELEVATION

SECTION

Erecting the bridge 558 ft (170 m) in the air was a major challenge (Figs.13,14). The key was providing heavy-lift capability. The system included eight electronically controlled center-hole hydraulic jacks with high-strength steel tendons running through them. Jack supports were cantilevered off the towers at level 55 and strapped back to the cores. Erection began with assembling the lower 4/5 of each leg on the ground. Legs were then lifted, placed vertically on their bearings and strapped to the tower columns (Fig.9).

This cleared the way for the bridge elements to follow. The central 80% of the walkway was assembled on the ground, with the top 1/5 of each leg bolted to the bridge crossbeam.

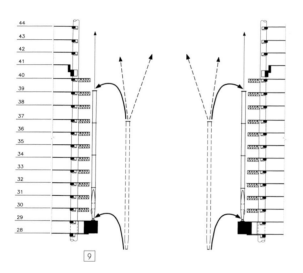

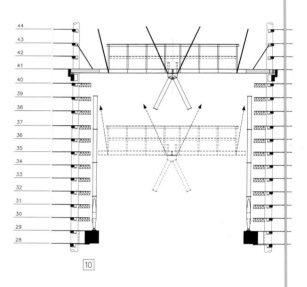

9 Before lifting the walkway, the lower 4/5 of the legs were assembled, lifted and placed on their bearings.

10 The central walkway with attached top 1/5 of legs was lifted on eight high-strength steel tendons, passing by previously placed lower legs and girder ends.

11 When lifted high enough, girder ends were hung from the walkway and welded to it.

12 When the arch legs were swung down in the last skybridge erection step, fabrication was so accurate that every bolt fit.

The walkway was then lifted in an intentionally slow and controlled procedure, a few meters an hour (Fig.10). After 48 hours of lifting, the walkway was in place; so bridge ends could be attached and lower legs swung into position and bolted (Figs.11,12).

The skybridge was completed with glass-and-stainless-steel façade panels, and a concrete-filled metal deck roof. The façade panels are tied to the top and the bottom walkway levels and use side joint travel to handle bridge flexing. Structurally, the bridge relies on the towers for gravity and lateral support, but allows them to move freely. This avoids the potentially damaging forces that can result when trying to restrain large moving buildings.

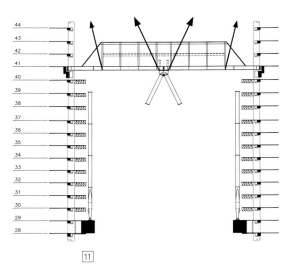

11

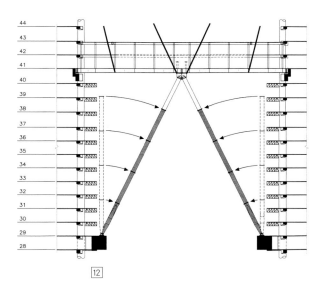

12

13 The central 325 ton (295 metric ton) portion of the skybridge walkway and top 1/5 of the arch legs were lifted as a unit in a three-day procedure.

14 As the skybridge walkway rose, the lower 4/5 of the arch legs could be seen above, temporarily "parked" against the towers.

31

Centre Court at Petronas Towers

The Kuala Lumpur City Centre includes Suria KLCC, a 1.5 million square foot (140,000 square meter) retail mall (Fig.6). Its focal point is a public space, the Centre Court, covered by a spectacular 18,800 square foot (1,750 square meter) domed roof. Architect Cesar Pelli's unique variations on dome design carefully control the quality of natural light entering the space. Instead of a circular footprint, roof geometry uses straight-line elements to cover an elliptical area. Instead of a continuous solid or glazed dome surface, this roof filters sunlight with alternating solid roof panels and radial skylight bands (Fig.4). In addition, each solid panel is stepped for clerestory windows that admit reflected light to brighten the ceiling surface. In a design irony, the "dome" is not a true dome: each panel is separate and trussed to create a lacy visual effect (Fig.7).

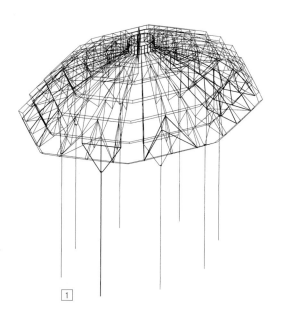

1

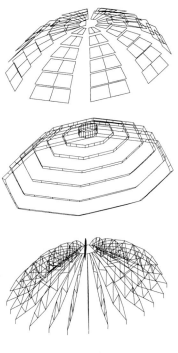

2

1 In the assembled structural framing model, circumferential steps occur atop the curved top chords of radial trusses; one set of trusses and one forked column are shown bold; triangular braces along the perimeter stabilize trusses and columns.

2 The four main elements of the Centre Court roof can be seen:
Solid roof panels have standing seam roofing on steel roof deck that spans circumferentially to radial short-span beams (not shown); skylights cover the radial gaps between roof segments.

Roof step Vierendeel trusses of rectangular steel tubes support the radial roof beams, delivering their load to radial trusses below; clerestory glazing admits indirect light through the steps.

Radial welded steel pipe trusses, balanced on forked columns, cantilever to a central cupola (not shown); their lower ends are pinned to a heavy concrete curb at the main mall roof.

Steel pipe forked columns supporting three radial trusses in each roof segment; below the fork, batten plates connect the three pipes for a single column continuing to grade.

The design team worked collaboratively to achieve Pelli's concept considering functionality, constructibility, and economy. Thornton-Tomasetti's innovative structural design uses eight triangular sectors, or "pie slices." Each consists of a main column, trusses, roof steps and deck (Figs.2,3). Two sets of trusses establish the geometry of all eight sectors. The roof membrane fastens to steel decking that bears on small radially oriented steel tubes. The tubes span between Vierendeel-trussed clerestories and cantilever outward to support sunshades. Six circumferential lines of Vierendeel trusses, supported by the curved top chords of double-tapered radial support trusses, create the roof's stepped profile (Fig.5).

Each of the eight "pie-slice" sectors is carried on three radial trusses balanced on a "forked" column: three steel pipes that meet and are linked by batten plates to work as a single unit. Each sector also has trusses and columns braced by triangles of struts anchored to the perimeter curb (Fig.1). The triple-columns extend downward, supporting retail mall floors below as well.

3 Roof Plan
A Steel roof deck spanning direction.
B Small radial beams and cantilevered sunshades.
C Radial skylights supported from solid roofs.
D Circumferential Vierendeel trusses.
E Radial main trusses.
F Forked columns.
G Ring curb and radial truss tiedown points.

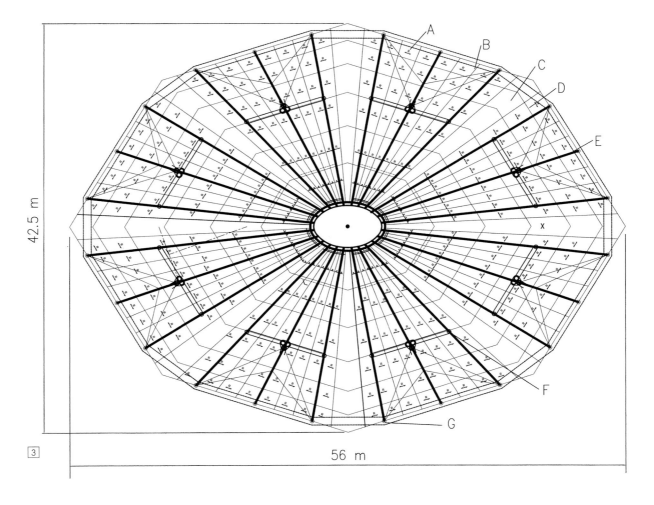

42.5 m

3

56 m

The column-supported truss approach allowed the roof to be constructed in individual segments and without the extensive scaffolding of a true dome. Each roof sector is restrained from tipping or shifting by connections to a structural concrete curb that rings the roof opening and spans roof loads to retail grid columns below.

4 Shade is inviting in tropical Malaysia, so the Centre Court dome mixes solid roofing and radial skylights.

5 The stepped profile of the Centre Court dome admits indirect sunlight to make the interior soffits glow. Rolling, telescoping ladders provide cleaning access.

6 The heart of Suria KLCC, the X-shaped shopping complex, is the elliptical Centre Court and adjacent crescent-shaped mall. The Concert Hall is located between the Petronas Towers 1 and 2.

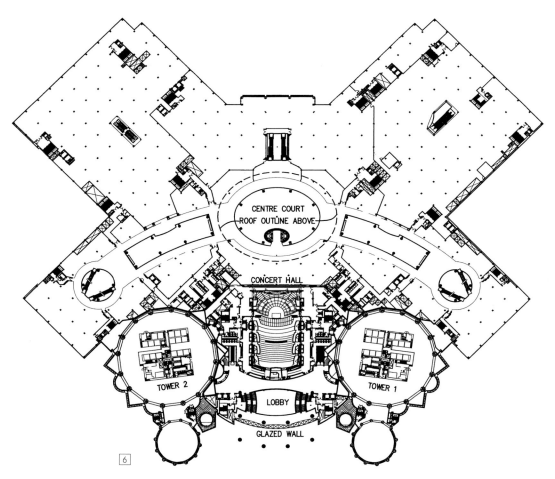

Unlike a true dome that can rise or sink slightly due to temperature changes, each balanced sector must grow or shrink radially and circumferentially. Pinned curb connections allow rotation and along-pin sliding movements. Support framing for radial skylights is bracketed off each sector, but sectors meet at flexible steel strips that keep them aligned while allowing circumferential "breathing room."

For a structural failure in any sector, the connections also permit load redistribution to neighboring sectors. The crowning touch is a cupola; its legs land on sector tips and flex to allow sector radial movement.

7 Uplighting at night dramatizes the lacy trusswork supports and rings of roof steps in the Centre Court dome.

Concert Hall at Petronas Towers

The Dewan Filharmonik Petronas Concert Hall, a world-class performance space, presented several unusual design challenges. Nestled between the Petronas Towers and surrounded by the Suria KLCC shopping mall, its location has no visibility and limited access for circulation. It is perched two floors above grade to clear a ground floor mall entry, and lands on a building grid skewed 45 degrees. A concourse-level meeting room below requires column-free space. The hall also needs acoustical isolation from the mall and from basement vehicular traffic.

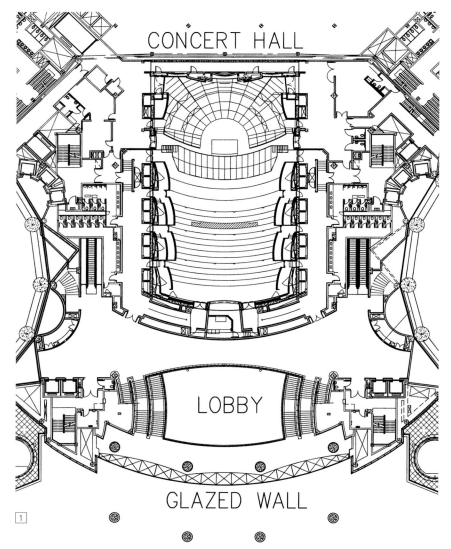

1 The Concert Hall fits snugly between the Petronas Towers, so its presence is indicated by a grand lobby visible from the street through a tall glazed wall.

The architectural solution to achieve visibility and circulation is a grand main lobby that serves as the concert hall lobby, as a link between the towers and as the ceremonial entrance to the whole KLCC complex. The Concert Hall is expressed and accessed by staircases that climb opposite lobby walls, by balconies at hall levels and by escalators and shuttle elevators (Fig.1). A curved glazed wall, braced by lacy steel rod trusses, encloses the chandelier-lit lobby and overlooks a formal garden outside (Figs.3,5,6).

The structural design solution to the other requirements is an ingenious "box within a box" that creates double walls and a double-slab floor. The "outer box" includes four concrete masonry walls surrounding the open space above a girder-supported lower floor slab. "Inner box" walls are concrete 1 ft (300 mm) thick and 100 ft (30 m) high. They are braced by parallel, vertical 3.3 ft (1 m) deep stiffening ribs. The "inner box" floor is the upper layer of the double slab. A ring of story-high girders support both "outer" walls and the "inner box," delivering their weight to columns on the skewed grid below and spanning over meeting rooms. The "box" roof uses concrete pavers and a membrane waterproofing system on a concrete-filled metal deck slab. It is carried by long-span steel trusses that bear on the "inner" walls (Fig.2).

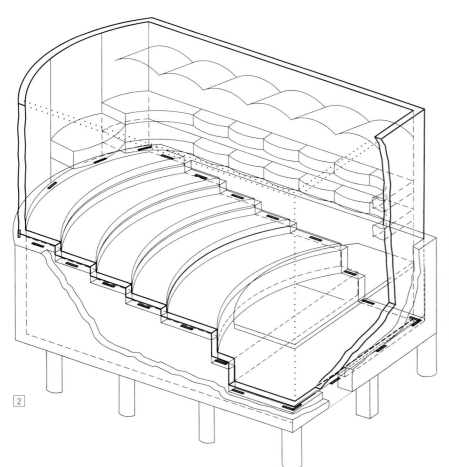

2 The Concert Hall is acoustically isolated from the rest of the Petronas Towers complex by "box within a box" construction: bold and dotted lines denote the inner box cut away to show the "inner box" floor and balconies. That box sits on thick rubber pads, shown as small rectangles, that bear on "outer box" girders and columns indicated by lighter lines.
Also note the double-slab stepped floor and the "inner box" stage and orchestra pit slabs.

3 The glazed front lobby wall, ceremonial entry for the whole Petronas complex, is supported by pretensioned trusses of thin steel rods.

Noise isolation was achieved using several strategies. Outdoor noises are blocked by the heavy roof slab. Structure-borne noise is blocked at the hall sides by a continuous, multi-story air gap between heavy "outer" and "inner" walls. Such gaps are simple to understand but difficult to construct, so inspection and mortar cleanout ports were left in the "outer" masonry, then filled after acoustician approval. At the floor, air gaps were simulated by soft spring supports. Between "inner" and "outer" floor slabs is a mat of soft batting with distributed rubber block springs. Where a double slab was impractical, an acoustical ceiling was spring-suspended from the "inner" floor (Fig.4). Building "inner box" walls was more challenging due to spring deflection of about 3/8 inch (10 mm). To avoid distortion, the walls were built on rigid blocks. Then the wall springs, laminated blocks of neoprene rubber and thin steel plate, were loaded by inflating flat jacks placed between them and the wall bottoms. Once jack forces lifted the walls slightly off the blocks, the jacks were permanently filled with grout and blocks were removed.

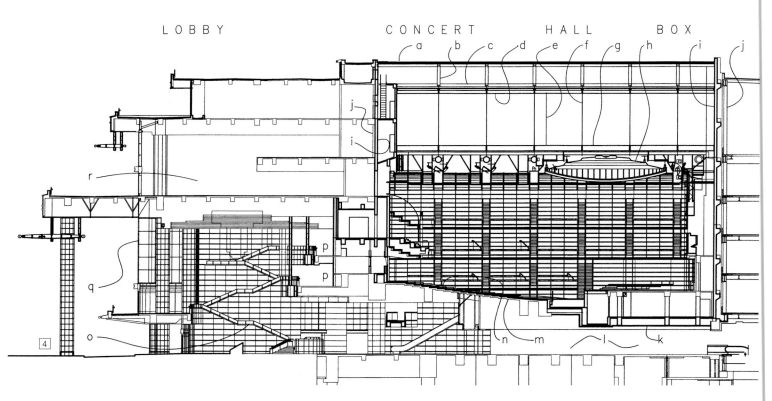

LOBBY   CONCERT   HALL   BOX

4 This sectional view cut through the long axis of the Concert Hall shows key elements of the Dewan Filharmonik design:

A Roof slab over the Concert Hall - it uses the mass of precast concrete roof pavers and a concrete-filled slab on metal deck to block noise from outside.

B Steel roof trusses span crosswise and bear on "inner box" concrete walls.

C Steel floor grid and catwalks brace and provide access to drive motors for adjustable acoustic ceiling.

D Rigid acoustic ceiling panels can be moved up or down to vary Concert Hall volume depending on the type of performance.

E Ceiling panel adjustment range is 23 ft (7 m).

F Hangers to fixed lower grid.

G Lower steel grid supports acoustically transparent, fixed architectural ceiling and lighting catwalks.

H Ceiling dome feature.

I "Inner box" concrete wall ("Inner box" concrete elements are shown bold).

J "Outer box" concrete masonry wall infill between concrete framing.

K Heavy spring-mounted acoustic isolation ceiling hung from "inner box" orchestra pit framing.

L Ground floor corridor to Suria KLCC shopping centre.

M "Outer box" stepped Concert Hall orchestra level floor slab.

N "Inner box" stepped floor slab on isolation mat of rubber pads and batt insulation.

O Lobby grand staircases.

P Lobby balconies hung from above.

Q Lobby glazed wall.

R Petroleum Science Museum space – "Petrosains" in Malayan.

The 885-seat Concert Hall is acoustically flexible, and can accommodate symphonic music as well as delicate Gamelan Malaysia performances (Fig.7). Above a perforated architectural ceiling, large, rigid, horizontal panels are suspended on motor-driven threaded rods. Raising or lowering the panels as much as 23 ft (7 m) changes the sound distribution, reverberation time and overall volume of the hall (Fig.8). In addition, concealed banners of sound-absorbing material can be positioned behind slotted wall panels or lifted clear of the performance hall. Pre-set combinations of panel and banner locations permit adjustment of Dewan Filharmonik Petronas acoustics at the push of a button.

8 Five elements of the Concert Hall are illustrated, from top down:
A Roof slab over the hall, isolated from surrounding roofs by a soft joint.
B Steel roof trusses supporting operable acoustic ceiling panels.
C Steel grid framing for the visible ceiling and lighting catwalks.
D "Inner box" concrete walls, balconies, upper stepped floor, stage and pit; black bars show rubber spring supports.
E "Outer box" surrounding walls, lower stepped floor and supporting columns.

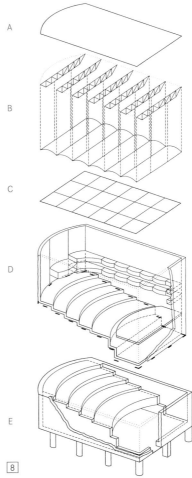

5,6 The presence of the Concert Hall is announced by a lobby with grand stairs and a sparkling chandelier (left) visible through a lacy glass wall (right).

7 The Dewan Filharmonik Petronas Concert Hall has a state-of-the-art interior with adjustable sound-damping panels concealed behind slotted wood wall panels, and operable acoustic ceiling panels concealed above an architectural ceiling with fiber optic illumination.

Miglin-Beitler Tower, Chicago

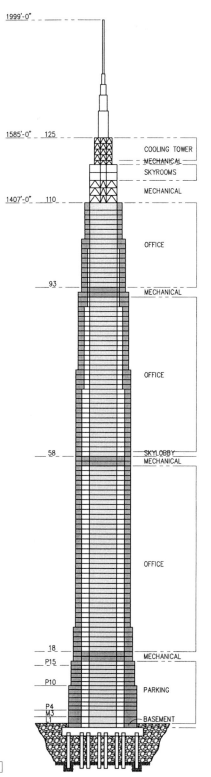

The Petronas Towers reflects a legacy of previous designs, especially the unbuilt Miglin-Beitler Tower. That skyscraper, proposed in 1989 for downtown Chicago, was to include 125 floors and a broadcast antenna reaching a record-breaking 2,000 ft (609.6 m) in height. Architect Cesar Pelli, engineer Thornton-Tomasetti, contractor Schal Associates and developers Lee Miglin and J. Paul Beitler collaborated and established the economic, construction and operations benefits of mixing high-strength concrete and steel-framed construction for high-rise buildings.

To fit the tight Chicago site, and to attract "boutique" office tenants by putting everyone near a window, floor plans were small. Because the tower was unusually slender, meeting the criteria for structural strength, stiffness, overturning resistance, and occupant comfort required an innovative design. Other design hurdles were retaining open views, meeting cost limits and building on a tight schedule. Locating major framing at the building perimeter is efficient for lateral strength and stiffness, but such designs affect façade architecture and block views. Examples include Sears Tower's steel "bundled tubes" and Hancock Center's steel "braced tube" systems in Chicago, and the former World Trade Center's steel "tubular frame" in New York.

The designers decided instead to use high-strength concrete – up to 14,000 psi (96 MPa) – which was practical thanks to recently developed admixtures and pozzolans (cement-like materials). Unlike steel, higher-concrete strength provides increased stiffness. Compared to a 6,000 psi (41 MPa) mixture widely used in the U.S., this concrete would be 133% stronger and 54% stiffer. As a result, it would be stiff enough to control wind sway when used in a core of concrete walls, linked to two large columns on each building face by outrigger walls and concrete floor girders (Fig.2).

1 Nominally just below the 2,000 ft (609.6 m) Federal Aviation Administration limit, the slender Miglin-Beitler Tower was to use concrete (shaded) to resist overturning by linking stepped outrigger columns with core walls through three sets of outrigger walls. Steel was to be used for infill floor framing and the tower top, housing broadcast and mechanical equipment.

Developer
Miglin-Beitler Development Company

Architect
Cesar Pelli & Associates, Inc.

Structural Engineer
Thornton-Tomasetti Engineers

Geotechnical Consultant
STS Consultants

Wind Consultant
Rowan Williams Davies & Irwin

General Contractor
Schal Associates

The inherent damping of concrete, about double that of an all-steel frame, would further reduce wind sway, and the mass of concrete framing would slow the sway rate down. As a result, occupants would be comfortable even in gusty conditions. The greater weight of concrete framing would also counteract uplift forces from overturning action in high winds, eliminating rock anchors or rock socket hold-downs. The concept of using a high-strength concrete core and perimeter for occupant comfort was applied later in the Petronas Towers.

Another Miglin-Beitler design feature appearing in the Petronas Towers was the combination of steel framing and concrete. For fast construction, typical floor framing for the Chicago structure was designed as a concrete-filled metal deck composite with steel beams. In addition, the top third of tower height, housing mechanical and broadcast equipment, was to have been steel-framed (Fig.1).

The Miglin-Beitler Tower design was an important step in the evolution of skyscrapers. The creative approaches developed for that unbuilt Chicago skyscraper were applied in the Petronas Towers at the end of the 20th century, and undoubtedly will be used in the 21st century as well.

2 This typical lower floor plan of the Miglin-Beitler Tower proposed for Chicago shows key aspects of the innovative design. Steel and concrete elements are mixed, using each where it is most effective.

A Massive outrigger columns of high-strength concrete project from each face, maximizing effective building width to resist overturning.

B Steel floor framing can be erected quickly between concrete core walls and columns.

C Concrete girders at every floor work with outrigger walls to link core and columns for overturning resistance.

D High-strength concrete core walls can rise quickly using self-climbing forms. The core resists a large fraction of wind and gravity loads.

E Perimeter steel spandrel beams and interrupted secondary columns deliver gravity load to outrigger columns.

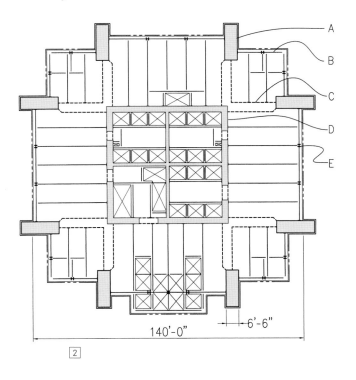

Random House, New York

A striking new tower has been designed by architects Skidmore, Owings & Merrill, Chicago/New York, for the publisher Random House in New York (Fig.1). The 50-story building combines the publisher's offices with luxury city residences above. The design delineates the tower's dual purposes through differing façades: the apartment levels have an all-glass curtain wall, while a façade of stone and steel distinguishes the office floors (Fig.2). The two areas are further defined by separate entrances, two setbacks, and jogs in the floor plans that create vertical setback ridges that increase the number of windows on the residential curtain wall, thereby maximizing views of the city's Central Park. These ridges also add texture to the tower surface.

1 The dual nature of Random House is clear from the change in floor size and cladding from the lower office levels to the upper residences. Vertical ridges visually link the two elements.

2 Lower floor façade panels framed with stone contrast with the smooth glass curtain wall used above and along the vertical ridges.

Beneath that façade lies a unique stacked structural system devised by Thornton-Tomasetti Engineers. Steel supports the office space on the lower 25 floors; the condominiums above have a concrete structural frame.

Working with SOM, the engineers used the most appropriate attributes of concrete and steel to realize the architect's vision. Steel-framed lower floors suited office usage by providing large column-free areas for efficient layouts and permitting easy future modifications for new floor openings or local heavy loads. Steel accelerated construction by its fast erection rate compared to concrete work, an important issue for a fast-track job (Fig.3).

3 Steel-framed office floors were erected quickly using two self-climbing tower cranes, one at the residential elevator shafts at building center and one standing in office elevator shafts to the side.

4 Above the trussed transition floor one crane was removed to permit concrete core construction. The other crane continued to rise alongside the residential floors. The trussed mechanical floor is visible before cladding installation.

Concrete was used for the upper floors to minimize floor-to-floor heights in residential construction, where ceiling ductwork is not needed and painted slab soffits can be used as ceilings. Concrete framing also allowed for more variation in apartment arrangements and sizes through shaping columns to suit. The reinforced concrete columns in this portion of the buildings vary in size, from 20 inches by 30 inches (508 mm by 762 mm), to 40 inches by 26 inches (1,016 mm by 660 mm), and in shape, from rectangular to square, to accommodate the architectural layouts. Column transfers at the 42nd floor to suit different layouts above resulted in a floor-to-floor height of 12 ft 8 inches (3.9 m) at that level, as compared to a typical height of 10 ft (3.1 m). These loads were transferred using concrete beams up to 30 ft (9.1 m) deep.

5 Steel-framed office floor legend:
A Spandrel beams moment-connected to columns form a perimeter lateral load-resisting frame.
B Steel-braced core surrounding elevator shafts for offices (top and bottom ends) and residences (middle).
C Cantilevered framing provides column-free corner offices with expansive views.

6 Elaborate steel framing is required at the transition between steel and concrete floors to handle irregular concrete column locations.
D Concrete core walls surrounding residential elevators and stairs.
F Concrete columns.
R Roof framing to each side of the central residential footprint.
T Trusses to pick up concrete columns and to form outriggers that engage perimeter columns to assist the braced core (all dashed lines are trussed).

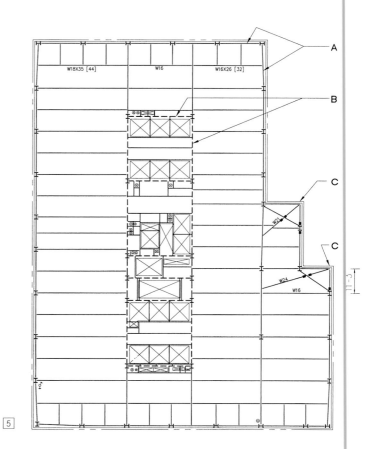

44

At steel-framed office floors, two of the ridge features continued down from the residential floors are carried on cantilevered framing, with moment-connected steel beams reaching out from interior girders to support the slab corner. This provided corner offices with dramatic panoramic views unobstructed by columns (Fig.5). The upper floors have concrete shear walls and slab moment-frames for lateral resistance. The designers accommodated shear walls within the varied apartment layouts and ceiling heights (Fig.7). Concrete placement was sped by retaining one of the two self-climbing tower cranes first used to erect the steel (Fig.4).

At steel-framed floors, lateral resistance is provided by a steel-braced core assisted by perimeter moment-frames and outriggers. Because the concrete columns and shear walls above do not correlate with the steel structural system below, the engineers devised an intricate transfer system at the 26th and 27th floors between the offices and the residential floors (Figs.6,8). At that level, the loads from the concrete stories are trans-

7 Concrete-framed residential floors have a stair-step outline to maximize views and an irregular column layout to suit the architectural floor plans.
D Concrete core walls surrounding residential elevators and stairs.
F Concrete columns.
S Concrete slab of 'flat-plate' construction with uniform thickness.
Crossing lines indicate locations and directions of major reinforcing bar groups.

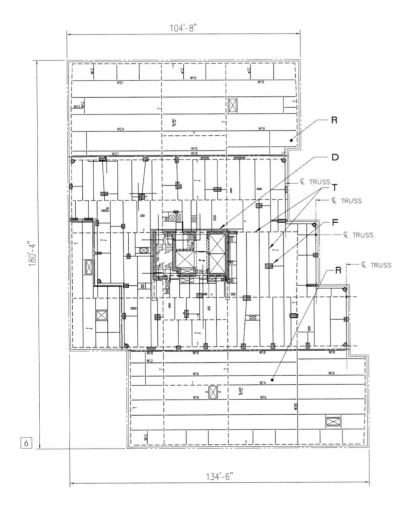

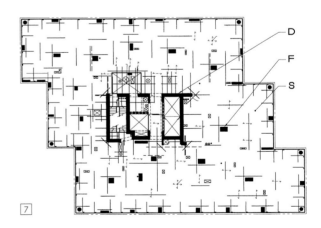

Random House, New York

mitted through steel girders to a complex of trusses that connect to the building's perimeter trusses (Figs.9,11). Together they act as outriggers, carrying both wind and gravity loads. The pickup girders used in the system range in depth from 55 inches (1,397 mm) to 87 inches (2,210 mm). The trusses have the economic advantage of keeping steel tonnage low and providing mechanical openings (Fig.12). Other column location shifts, from lobby to office floors, were provided economically by sloping the columns within the lower mechanical room (Fig.10). The sloping columns addressed

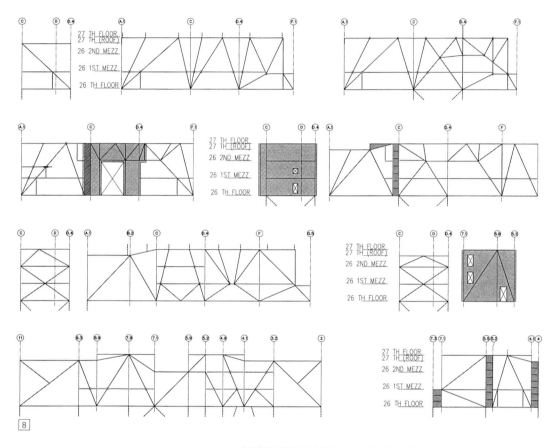

8

8 Complex truss arrangements support upper concrete columns (stubs above trusses), transition from steel-braced core to concrete shear walls (shaded segments) and engage outer columns for overturning resistance.

9 Perimeter trusses create outrigger and belt truss behavior for lateral resistance.

setback requirements and avoided the steel costs of large, heavy pickup girders. To minimize the slope and the horizontal thrust, most columns slope from the fifth to the second floor.

During construction, it was imperative to monitor and control the stresses on the steel system as loads from above accumulated. The engineers calculated loads at each step of the process to determine how the concrete would settle on the steel. During the actual process, they monitored the loads, ready to offset any imbalance swiftly.

10 To accommodate architectural requirements at the lobby level, some columns slope within the second floor mechanical room to the regular office floor grid.

11 Truss geometry varies to work with columns above.

12 Truss layouts still allow for passage of mechanical equipment at the transition floor.

Random House, New York

The design team was also concerned about occupant comfort at the upper levels. After study, they selected tuned liquid column dampers, devices used in Europe, but not previously in the U.S. Less costly than other dampers, the custom-made damper system uses water oscillating in two large water-filled U-shaped concrete tanks, each 20 ft (6.1 m) wide, 12 ft (3.7 m) tall and up to 70 ft (21.3 m) long (Fig.15). The tanks are set at right

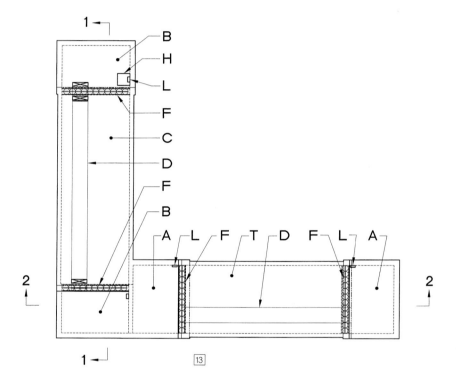

13 This plan shows location of elements at all levels, including turbulence-inducing screens, air transfer ducts and slabs over tunnels and upstands.

angles to damp both north-south and east-west motions (Fig.14). Vertical screens across the horizontal bottom segments of the U tanks generate turbulence that provides the damping action (Fig.13). The proportions of the tanks differ, following a design based on theoretical structural analyses and work with wind-tunnel experts. The damper's weight dictated a steel frame above the 49th floor.

The Random House building opened in late 2002.

Owner/Developer
The Related Companies LP

Architect (Core & Shell)
Skidmore, Owings & Merrill LLP

Architect (Office Interior)
HLW International LLP

Architect (Residential)
Ismael Leyva Architects

Architect (Residential Lobby)
Adam D. Tihany International Ltd.

Structural Engineer
Thornton-Tomasetti Engineers

Construction Manager
Plaza Construction Corp.

Other Team Members

Mechanical, Electrical & Plumbing Engineer
Cosentini Associates
Geotechnical Engineer
Langan Engineering
Site & Subway Engineer
Vollmer Associates
Steel Erector & Fabricator
ADF Steel Corp.
Concrete Contractor – Foundation
Urban Foundation / Engineering LLP
Concrete Contractor – Superstructure
North Side Concrete Corp.
Testing Lab
Delta Testing Laboratories, Inc.
Concrete Mix Supplier (Foundation)
Ferrara Brothers Concrete Co.
Concrete Mix Supplier (Superstructure)
Quadrozzi Concrete Corp.

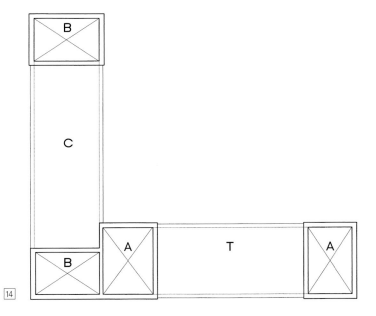

14 This plan cut just above the connecting tunnels shows upstands for the two U-shaped tanks.

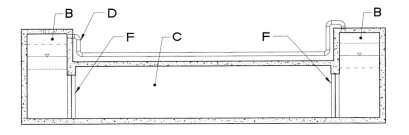

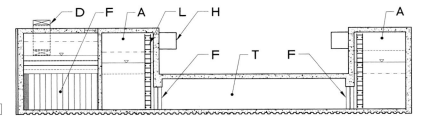

15 U-shaped concrete water tanks act to help damp building motions in windy conditions to improve occupant comfort. Water oscillates between the upstanding legs through the connecting tunnel, passing through screens that create turbulence. Two tank cross-sections are shown here, 1-1 at top and 2-2 below.
A Upstanding legs for east-west tank.
B Upstanding legs for north-south tank.
C Connecting tunnel for north-south tank.
D Duct for air transfer between upstands as water rises and falls.
F 'Fence' or screen to create turbulence as water oscillates.
H Hatch for inspection access.
L Ladder for inspection access.
T Connecting tunnel for east-west tank.

The New York Times Building, New York

When architect Renzo Piano designed the new headquarters of The New York Times, he envisioned a bright tower "floating off into the air." His 52-story building, wrapped by off-white ceramic screens, is a serene oasis in New York City's densely populated Times Square area (Fig.1). Steel, glass and ceramic elements work together to create the impression of lightness. Upper floors cantilever beyond the ground floor building face to enhance the effect.

The new building has an unusually high profile, both due to the prominence of the newspaper and that of the design architect. The building's architecture is largely expressed through exposed steel framing. "New York City has rarely seen exposed steel on this scale," says Daniel Kaplan of Fox & Fowle, the local architect. Kaplan likened the project to craft building. "Nothing in the design is solely ornamental," he says, "the structure tells the story of how the building stands."

1 Color, ceramic screens, exposed bracing and building overhangs create an impression of lightness for The New York Times Building.

The building has a simple and symmetric structural steel skeleton without setbacks (Fig.2). A central braced core and outrigger system can resist all lateral loads. Three east-west braced frames extend the full building height. Two north-south braced frames extend from grade to the 28th floor mechanical room, and a single north-south braced frame splits the elevator banks from 28th floor to building top. Outrigger trusses at the 28th floor and at the rooftop extend from the core to engage all perimeter columns. The repetitive and symmetrical floor framing ensured economical fabrication and erection (Fig.3).

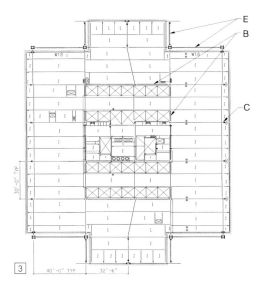

2 Large notches at each corner create narrow building faces to enhance visual slenderness and height. The overhangs are also visible in this view.

3 Key features of the building are shown in this typical lower floor plan. Core bracing (B) on three east-west lines continues full height. Two north-south bracing lines transition to a single centerline brace at upper floors. On east and west faces floors cantilever slightly beyond columns (C), while cantilevered north and south bays are supported by exterior bracing (E) and an interior "ladder frame."

Each corner of the tower floor plan is notched, and within the notches prominent X-bracing rises from the tower base to its roof. Behind the steel bracing, glass panels offer a symbolic nod to journalistic transparency. The eight sets of braced panels within the notches form highly visible architectural accents between the ceramic-screened exterior glass curtain walls (Fig.6).

4 Full-scale mock-ups were used to study the ceramic rod screens and building enclosure used for the façade between corner notches.

5 Ceramic rod screens continue upward past the building enclosure to simultaneously conceal rooftop equipment and reinforce the desired impression of lightness as the building appears to float off into the air.

6 At corner notches, the building façade uses fritted glass panels (W) behind the exposed steel bracing for physical and metaphorical transparency. Convenience stairs (Z) linking newspaper office floors are visible behind the glass.

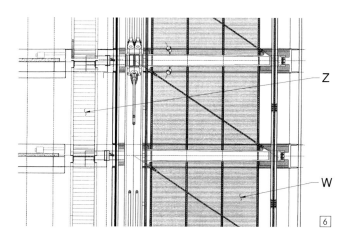

Z

W

The screens consist of parallel horizontal ceramic tubes that sit 1.6 ft (0.5 m) beyond the building skin and extend above the roof line (Figs.4,5). They add texture and lightness, while saving energy by shading occupants (Fig.8). Behind the main tower is a five-story podium with a garden atrium open to the sky (Fig.7). A vast newsroom at the lower levels has columns on 30 ft by 40 ft (9.1 m by 12.2 m) bays, and the ground floor has retail space.

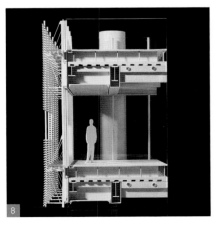

7 The New York Times Building includes an adjacent podium building with garden atrium open to the sky.

8 The complex relationships between the ceramic screen, the glazed enclosure behind it, and the ceiling sandwich of raised floor, structural framing and ceiling space was studied by numerous models and drawings.

Renzo Piano's wish to retain the drama of exposed X-braced steel presented a fireproofing quandary. Thornton-Tomasetti Engineers, the consulting engineers for the tower, helped realize the architect's vision. By designing the framework so that the function of exposed bracing was limited to enhancing occupant comfort, minimizing deflections and accelerations, they showed that fire protection was not needed there for building safety. So the bracing rods are clean and crisp, says Kaplan.

The bracing was exquisitely detailed by Piano, down to specifying button head bolts. Detailed wooden models were used to study esthetics and construction access (Fig.10). A full-scale steel model of a complex bracing joint was then fabricated to confirm the esthetic intent as well as to instruct the fabricators and designers (Figs.11,12,13).

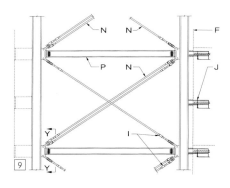

9 The four bays of east-west X-bracing exposed at building corners did not require fireproofing, as they supplement the outrigger-stiffened core bracing lateral load resisting system but are not required to meet building strength criteria. This typical two-story-tall panel shows key features.
Legend for all bracing drawings:
A Single steel rods carry each floor framing level at building overhangs.
B Tapered built-up welded steel beam carries north and south end bay framing.
C Connection plate links story-high double-channel members through high-strength bolts.
D Back to back MC 10 x 33.6 (254 mm x 50 kg/m) steel channels.
E Spacer plates between double channels.
F Face of the building enclosure envelope; bracing is outside.
G Steel box column built up from plates.
H Field-welded moment connection at beam end braces the exposed column.
I Cylindrical length-adjusting sleeve on each rod is snugged after rod is jacked to specified tension.
J Jog or vertical offset in floor beams sets protruding beam ends at elevations to match bracing struts.
K Stiffener within the box column.
L Raised flooring in office spaces.
M Office floor concrete-filled slab on metal deck.
N Twinned high-strength steel rods; one pair is oriented horizontally and the other vertically to pass by at the intersection point.
P Horizontal steel strut completes the X-bracing load path and resists compression from rod pretensioning.
Q Closure plates are set and field-welded after beam-end bolted connections are completed.
R A shimmed and sealed gap at each beam end permits field adjustment for construction variations within acceptable tolerance criteria.
S Feature strip of steel.
T Horizontal stiffener as beam stub flange.

10 This large-size wooden mock-up was used to study esthetics and construction access conditions at the exterior rod bracing joints.

11 A full-size steel joint was fabricated to study appearance and construction issues. The photo shows how connection gusset plates are contoured to meet the architect's vision.

12 The upper gusset is built up from multiple plates, as shown in this close-up of the full-size steel sample joint.

13 With bracing rod stubs connected to the gussets by single-sided "spade" and double-sided clevis connections, the full-size steel sample joint is complete in this photo.

The steel rods forming two-story X-braces in exterior panels are woven together in precise patterns: two rods oriented side-by-side straddle two crossing rods oriented over-and-under (Fig.9). All rod ends connect to paddle-shaped gusset plates prewelded to the tower's exterior box columns, along with a highly detailed stub to receive field-bolted bracing beams (Figs.15,16). To remain taut and functional during load reversals, each rod is tensioned in place with jacks. The resulting length change is taken up by a sleek sleeve rather than a conventional turnbuckle. To work with the exterior bracing module, floor beam ends are offset where they penetrate the curtain wall and connect to exposed columns (Fig.14). The highly visible steel corner columns are four-plate boxes with expressed flange tips. They are spliced to tight tolerances, following Piano criteria.

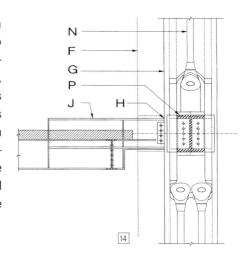

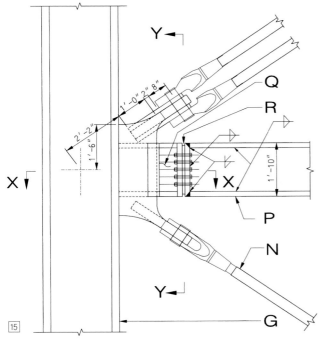

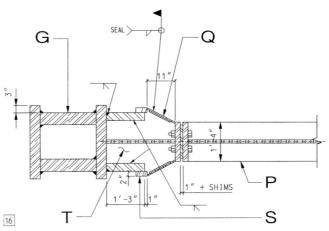

14 Beam ends jog upward within the raised floor space, penetrating the façade at elevations that match the bracing struts. Protruding beam ends are insulated to control steel temperatures and condensation points.

15 A close-up of the bracing joint shows careful detailing of all elements.

16 Plan section XX through the bracing joint shows an exposed box column with projecting flange tips and a boxed-out beam stub.

Thornton-Tomasetti's understanding of constructibility and the need for visual coherence was a true asset in the bracing design and fabrication, says Kaplan. Because of the "unity of visual and structural function," there was extraordinary collaboration on the project. According to David Thurm, the New York Times Vice President for Real Estate Development, the engineers were willing to "tweak and retweak" the design to achieve the most cost-effective translation of the architectural demands. For example, the north and south ends have no columns to obstruct the first floor entry area (Fig.17). Their corners are supported by expressed diagonals on every floor (Fig.18). At mid-face, a vertical ladder frame carries the load back to the tower, but it would not be effective until multiple floors were erected and welded. Thornton-Tomasetti devised temporary struts to support the cantilevered overhang without hampering construction. They also provided systems to resist progressive collapse in the event of unforeseen damage, a recent design mindset in the city.

17 Overhanging building bays visible in this view of the model are carried by diagonal braces and vertical ladder frames.

18 Cantilevered end bays have multiple parallel support systems, including diagonal rods, continuous vertical hangers and cantilever moment connections on the exposed tapered floor beams. See p.54, Fig.9 for legend.

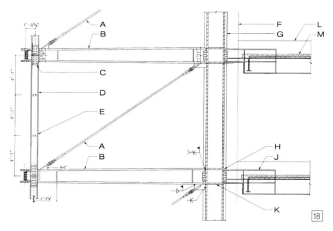

On most projects, detailed design of the concealed building frame and the visible architectural elements can proceed on related, but parallel, tracks. On this project, where the structure forms much of the architecture, collaboration had to be much more extensive: the engineers had to understand and be sensitive to the architectural intent of structural members and details, and the architects had to respect and accommodate the requirements imposed by physics and construction realities on the exposed structure. Considering the level of coordination needed, the project schedule was compressed: less than one year from design to bidding. The engineers produced highly-detailed design development documents, the result of many studies that will save the owners money in the long run, says Rob Willis, Vice President at Forest City Ratner, the building's co-owners and developers.

The new headquarters building is topped by a 300 ft (91.4 m) tall, tapering, slender mast that "climbs off into the sky," in Piano's words (Fig.19). The designers for this "symbol of lightness," that visually transitions from the solidity of the building to the sky, had to find the right balance among the competing demands of cost – including the effect of the mast on the building below – and appearance, durability, material availability, fabrication techniques and erection methods. Exhaustive engineering studies of prospective mast designs were conducted by many parties, including wind tunnel consultants, to find that balance.

Extraordinary care with details was evident throughout the design and construction process. Even nearly hidden framing that supports the ceramic screen above the roof line was thoroughly analyzed. Thornton-Tomasetti Engineers examined many variables, looking at cantilevered and braced columns, straight and various tapered profiles, and solid and perforated webs, to achieve the architect's esthetic standards without losing sight of cost and structural integrity at all times.

The New York Times Building opens in 2006.

Owner
The New York Times Company and Forest City Ratner Companies

Architect
Renzo Piano Building Workshop and Fox & Fowle Architects P.C.

Structural Engineer
Thornton-Tomasetti Engineers

New York Times Interior Architect
Gensler

Development Consultant
The Clarett Group

Owner's Representatives
Gardiner & Theobald, Inc.

Construction Manager
AMEC Construction Management, Inc.

Other Team Members

Mechanical, Electrical & Plumbing Engineer
Flack + Kurtz
Geotechnical Engineer
Mueser Rutledge Consulting Engineers
Acoustical Consultant
Cerami & Associates
Steel Fabricator
Havens/Interstate Iron Works
Steel Erector
Interstate Iron Works

19

19 A slender mast is part of the design concept, to gradually transition from the building to the sky.

Times Square Tower, New York

The site for the Times Square Tower in New York posed almost every constraint possible in urban construction. The tower is 49 stories high with a trapezoidal footprint of only 22,300 square feet (2,070 square meters) in the heart of New York's densely populated theater district, an extremely high-profile location. Because of the area's history and celebrity, the city created an oversight body, the 42nd Street Development Corporation. In addition to the small site, Architect David Childs of SOM, New York, had to hew to criteria set by the corporation as to building's height, usable floor space, setbacks, mechanical spaces and signage. Below-ground conditions were also restrictive, a thicket of subway tunnels and stations (Fig.4).

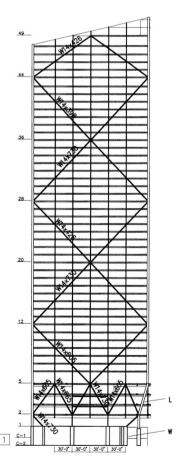
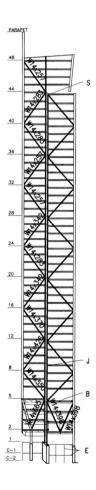

1 Bracing elevations for (left to right) east, north, west and south building faces have different patterns to suit the different building face widths and column spacing. Note the north (second) elevation right half is intentionally displaced right and down to highlight the jog or offset along that wall.

Left-hand member sizes also apply to corresponding right-hand members.

B Brackets for elaborate Times Square style signage between second and fifth floor.
E Existing 1890's steel framing retained and encased in concrete.
J Jog or offset in the north elevation.
L Leaning columns open ground floor access at the northeast corner.
W Walls of cast-in-place concrete deliver lateral loads from bracing to foundations.

2 West and south bracing elevations use different modules to avoid common nodes that would block corner office views. HSS 12 indicates square steel tubing, 12 inches (305 mm) wide.

In spite of the obstacles, the new mixed-use tower is an "incredibly tall building, elegant and slender," says Christopher Fogarty of Fogarty Architects, New York, formerly of SOM, who continued to work on the project after he set up his own consultancy. SOM architect Carl Galioto says the integration of architecture and structural engineering is always important, and more so in a tall, narrow high-rise. The aspect ratio (height/width of structural frame) for this building would have been 22 if the structural system to resist lateral loads had been restricted to the building core. This would have been too high to be practical or cost-effective (Fig.3). After studying many options, the engineers designed a braced tube structural system that reduced the lateral system aspect ratio to between 9 and 5.4, depending on load direction (Figs.1,2).

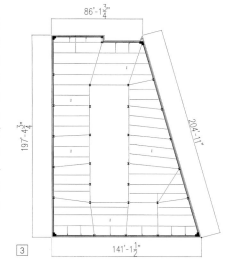

3 This typical floor plan shows the trapezoidal overall building shape, north face jog, skewed framing between core and perimeter column layouts, typical wide-flange I-shaped columns and solid steel L-shaped corner columns. The central area is shown blank since elevator and stair framing varies on different floors.

4 At the busiest spot in New York City, the trapezoidal site is surrounded by subway tunnels and stations, requiring extraordinary design and coordination efforts.

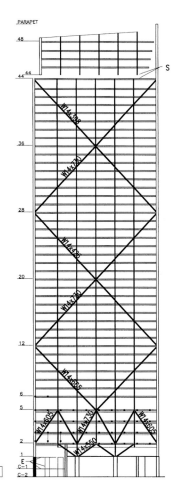

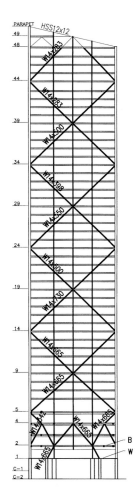

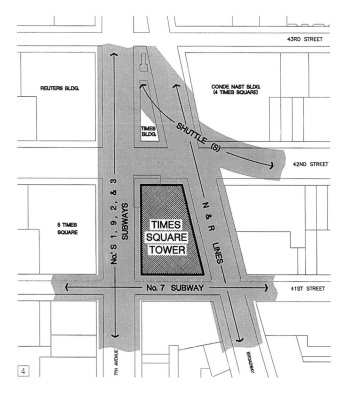

Bracing forms giant X's on each of the building faces, with the height of the X defining the bracing module. On the east and west sides of the tower, each X-brace is 16 stories high, on the south side the bracing modules encompass ten stories, and on the narrow north face, the bracing forms an X every eight stories (Fig.9).

The design intent was to express the structure while providing maximum floor space. The beauty of working with Thornton-Tomasetti Engineers was their familiarity with tall buildings, says Fogarty, "they understood the structural logic of the bracing and produced a rigorous design, with no excess."

The bracing system is partially expressed on the narrow (90 ft, 27.4 m) north side of the tower, a focal point on Manhattan's 42nd Street (Fig.6). It was also complicated by an offset that splits the wall (Fig.5). Half of each X is highlighted on the façade, creating a visual "zipper" linking the "jazzy" Times Square side and the calmer corporate side of the building. The tone

5 The narrow north building face appears even more slender due to an offset in the face that defines two different façade treatments.

6 One half of the north face bracing system is expressed on the cladding, providing a "jazzy" face on Times Square.

of these façades lies in the cladding design. Large diagonal bracing is also expressed within the Broadway entry on the east side of the tower, where visitors pass through a five-story glass atrium.

The Times Square Development Corporation mandates paradoxically guided the structural solution. The corporation does not consider tower-top mechanical spaces in determining building height limits, an anomaly in New York and an advantage for the owners. Putting all mechanical rooms at the top maximized open retail and other rentable space, but precluded using a braced core with outriggers to the building perimeter at mid-height mechanical floors.

The owner's desire to limit window obstructions also affected the structural system design. By establishing X-bracing modules that do not meet neatly at the building's corners, the design team avoided corner offices with window obstructions on both faces (Figs.7,8).

9 X-braces on the east and west building faces follow a 16-story module.

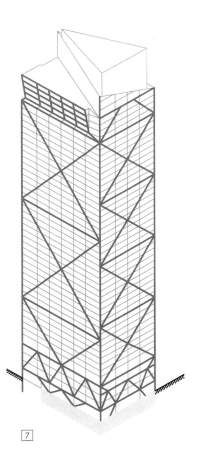

7

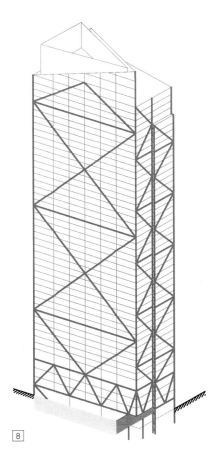

8

7 The south and west faces of Times Square Tower are braced by X-braces that cover several floors, and intentionally do not meet at corners.

8 North and east building faces present a complex pattern. The east face is similar to the west, but the north includes a jog in planes. Also note the open spaces at ground level.

10 Corner columns are solid steel L-shapes built up from steel plates 5.5 inches (140 mm) thick, welded together.

11 Main building L-shaped columns have legs oriented to follow building faces. This plan shows the variation in column size from bottom to top for one column line.

This decision increased force transfers at the columns and complicated connections to the floors, the building corners and the diagonals. To further reduce visual obstructions, the corner columns were made as compact as possible by building them up from stacked steel plate (Fig.10). Column sizes also shrink at upper floors as axial loads reduce (Fig.11). The steel fabricator devised joints 22 inches (559 mm) thick of welded steel plates with stubs welded on at the shop (Figs.12,13). In the field, the members were joined by a mix of welding and bolting (Fig.17).

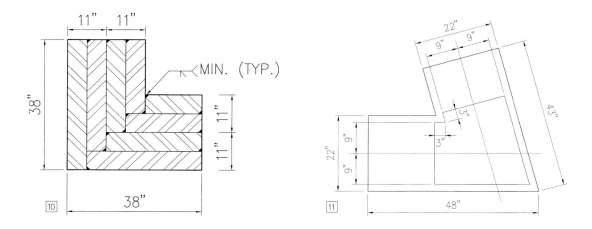

12 To transmit tremendous bracing forces through joints, the fabricator stacked steel plates to create solid nodes, and shop-welded stubs to them to receive bracing members.

13 Bracing joints awaiting members.

The engineers contributed to solving complex foundation problems, calculating where to place columns in the maze of subway tunnels to minimize interference with construction (Fig.14). The partial foundation of an 1890 building in the northeast corner was another design factor (Figs.15,16).

14 Some columns penetrated through the subway corridors after careful coordination with the Transit Authority.

15 Below-grade steel framing from a century-old building was preserved in some key locations to minimize disturbance to adjacent transit structures.

16 Existing steel framing was encased within new concrete walls that transmit building gravity and lateral forces to deep foundations.

17 This connection includes a column that turns to become a brace and projecting plates for other member connections, creating an abstract sculptural appearance.

The structural design transfers most of the building weight to the tower's massive corner columns that transfer to caissons. However, to enhance building access one corner column was eliminated. Instead the engineers provided a split column system: two columns, set back at the base, gradually slope outward and merge to become one column at the fifth level where the building's main lobby begins. The owners also wanted to minimize the number of ground level columns that might interfere with retail space, so a belt truss picks up alternating perimeter columns, ties the structural system together and compensates for fewer perimeter columns below. The truss is concealed behind the three-story signage band mandated by the Development Corporation.

Core columns carry only gravity loads, with minimal bracing to avoid interfering with rentable space. Perimeter steel columns are shaped, up to 4 ft (1.2 m) wide. On one corner, at the ground floor the steel lands on a 5 ft 3 inch (1.6 m) square column of 12,000 psi (83 MPa) concrete. Loads from the other three steel columns are spread along the tops of buttressed foundation walls.

18 To protect New York City subway tunnels that are deeper than the building basement, column loads are transferred to rock below the tunnel level by groups of high-capacity caissons. The caissons also resist uplift.
A Property line adjacent to subway.
B Steel column built up from stacked plates.
C First floor concrete slab.
D Original rock surface before excavation.
E Y-shaped steel base plate to distribute column load among three caissons.
F Dywidag high-strength rods to hold down base plate against uplift.
G Steel ring lugs for core-to-Dywidag load transfer.
H Rock socket of caisson.
I Heavy steel pipe shell with bond breaker to avoid loading upper rock.
J Annular space filled with 10,000 psi concrete.
K 13 inches (330 mm) diameter solid steel core with lugs for core-to-socket load transfer.
S Sidewalk.
T Tunnel roof over subway.
U Street.
V Subway tunnel lower track slab.

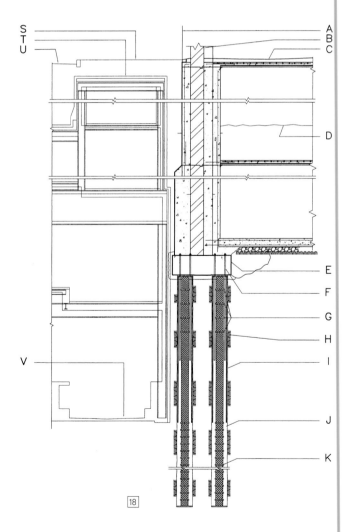

The south side of the building has two subway levels below ground, a full story below the rest of the site (Fig.18). A single caisson, sized per code for the building's loads, would have come within 6 inches (152 mm) of the tunnels. Working with outside consultants, Thornton-Tomasetti proposed using three smaller caissons, each 24 inches (610 mm) in diameter at each of the south corners (Fig.19). Steel cores carry loads down past the subways (Fig.20). A custom-designed steel plate distributes the loads of the massive corner columns among the caissons below (Fig.21). By minimizing interference with subway operation and allowing the contractors to use conventional equipment for this side of the foundation, money and time were saved. The caissons also connect to the base plate through high-strength hold-down rods, and then to columns through field welds, to resist uplift forces from the columns and the steel diagonals. In addition, foundation walls are engaged by shear studs along the embedded columns (Fig.22).

Times Square Tower opened in early 2004, taking a prominent place among the group of new skyscrapers that have transformed the city's theater district over the last decade.

Owner / Developer
Boston Properties

Architect
Skidmore, Owings & Merrill LLP

Structural Engineer
Thornton-Tomasetti Engineers

Construction Manager
Turner Construction Co.

Other Team Members

Mechanical, Electrical & Plumbing Engineer
Jaros Baum & Bolles
Site / Civil Engineer
Vollmer Associates LLP
Geotechnical Consultant
Mueser Rutledge Consulting Engineer
Steel Fabricator
Canron Construction Co.
Steel Erector
Canron Construction Co.

19 Three narrow caissons were used under one column to minimize disturbance to adjacent subway tunnels.

20 Cylindrical cores of solid steel with shear-transfer rings were lowered into holes drilled for the deep caissons to minimize caisson diameters and avoid subway tunnels.

21 A custom steel base plate distributes the load of an L-shaped corner column to three caissons below.

22 Corner L-shaped columns of solid steel engage encasing concrete foundation walls through shear studs, as well as bearing on base plates over caissons.

Bank One Corporate Center, Chicago

Chicago's new Bank One Corporate Center relies on both hidden and visible structural innovations. Hidden is its re-use of century-old foundations: belled caissons from an 1892 building (Fig.1). In 1986, that building was torn down leaving the old foundation in the ground. The prime downtown site lay idle for years, the cost of removing the caissons discouraging potential developers. Thornton-Tomasetti Engineers found a way to adapt the old foundation, making new construction economically viable.

The new 37-story office building fronts Dearborn Street, with an 11-story retail bustle on State Street, a major Chicago shopping area. Ricardo Bofill of Barcelona was the architectural design consultant for building massing, exterior and lobby design, and DeStefano + Partners of Chicago was the Architect of Record. The owner and the entire design team undertook an intense 60-day assessment of the proposed project. According to Ray Clark, DeStefano's President, the engineer's innovative structural approach was a major factor in making the project possible.

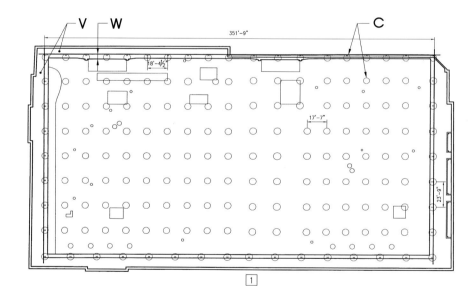

1

1 Belled caissons and a perimeter foundation wall
from an 1892 building were "buried treasure"
to the developer of Bank One Corporate Center,
dramatically reducing foundation costs.
C Existing caisson locations on an existing grid of
  approximately 18 ft by 24 ft (5.5 m by 7.3 m).
V Existing sidewalk vault.
W Existing full-depth foundation wall.

The foundation solution involved distributing loads from new columns onto existing caissons in different locations. First, a new transfer mat was cast on the existing basement slab on grade. By using 10,000 psi (69 MPa) concrete and heavy reinforcing, the concrete mat was sufficiently thin – only 48 inches to 54 inches (1,219 mm to 1,372 mm) thick – to leave space for three basement levels as the owner requested (Fig.2). Then, to deliver high-rise column loads to caissons under foundation walls, the walls were partially removed and replaced with 6 ft (1.8 m) wide, story-deep concrete cap beams (Fig.3).

And finally, smaller low-rise column loads were delivered to under-wall caissons by landing them on wall panels doweled to the inside face of existing foundation walls.

2 Several structural methods were used to transfer new column loads to the old caisson grid while distributing loads to avoid overloading any one caisson.
A Additional concrete doweled to the existing foundation wall to support new columns in off-wall locations.
B Buttresses to distribute new column loads at their tips among several existing caissons below.
C Existing caisson locations on an existing grid of approximately 18 ft by 24 ft (5.5 m by 7.3 m).
E New elevator walls spread core gravity and lateral loads among caissons below.
P New concrete pilaster connected to existing foundation wall.
S Shear reinforcing stirrups cast into the new foundation mat to permit use of a thin mat that preserves basement headroom (all shaded, outlined areas).
W Existing full-depth foundation wall.

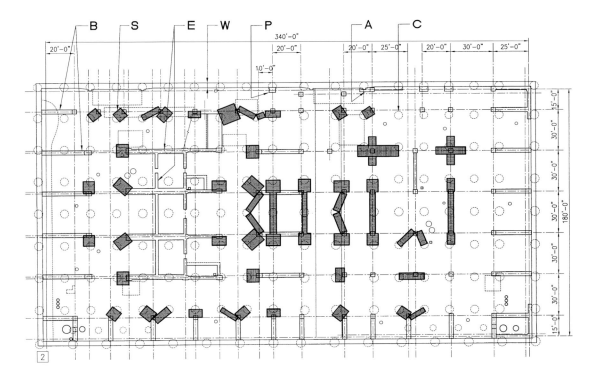

3 In some locations, new deep cap beams were cast to replace foundation walls and distribute perimeter column loads to existing caissons.

A more visible innovation was used to overcome another development obstacle: an original column grid that did not conform to current high-rise practice. If the engineers had simply extended the old column grid up through the building, open floor space would have been severely curtailed. Thornton-Tomasetti Engineers devised a sloped column system, taking advantage of a Chicago code provision that allows buildings to project over the public right-of-way above a certain height. Between the third and fifth floors, some columns lean outward as far as 9 ft (2.7 m) (Figs.4,5). Above, columns rise over the sidewalk, providing ample column-free space on upper floors (Fig.6). Below, loads are close to the old column grid. By tilting columns symmetrically on opposite building faces, gravity loads are balanced. Transferring forces around slab openings also required horizontal, under-floor trusswork.

4 Sloping columns are used to gain additional floor space above the sidewalk right-of-way, following Chicago building regulations.
B Stainless steel braces from floor to lobby façade.
E Architectural enclosures of sloping column.
F Raised floor for wiring access.
G Glazed façade planes.
R Revolving door to lobby.
S Sloping steel column.

5 Sloping columns provide more interior space on upper floors.

E

S

F

14' – 6"

14' – 6"

G

20' – 0"

B

R

27' – 0"

As the steel transfer system had to handle not just vertical gravity loads, but also their effect as horizontal forces towards and away from the building, and parallel to the building face to pass around floor openings, its analysis and design was complex and involved some massive connections. Still, the design was much more economical than the other approaches studied, such as cantilever supports for each floor.

Another innovation are the 14 inch (356 mm) raised mechanical floors with plenum space for state-of-the art wiring and for air distribution that allows individualized temperature control. The system also afforded construction economies. The engineers could support the floors with slightly larger, but fewer, steel beams placed 15 ft (4.6 m) apart. This meant fewer beams to erect, saving time, and less overall steel, saving cost. The raised floors also allow for construction flexibility; contractors do not have to achieve laser-level flatness because the prefabricated floors are adjustable to deliver a flat surface.

6 During construction the curved façade bay clearly showed how column offsets were handled by outward-sloping columns.

The façades at Bank One Corporate Center are reflective, high-performance, low emissivity glass. To break up the mass, the surfaces have horizontal feature bands of polished and satin-finish steel. Similar vertical steel bands climb the structure's corners, topped by tear-drop-shaped steel caps. The outward sloped column frame was transformed into curving bays that break up the surface on all four sides of the office tower and three sides of the retail bustle. The State Street entrance is a recessed rectangle leading to the retail area that continues below ground and connects to area airports via rapid transit. The lobby uses structural glazing to dramatic effect, with vertical glass mullions restrained by exposed pinned connections (Figs.7,8,9). Bank One Corporate Center opened in 2002.

7 Exterior columns stand in front of the glazed wall, permitting an uninterrupted shimmering plane to pass by.

8 The glass mullions are hung from above, and laterally restrained near ground level by stainless steel pin details.

9 The dramatic lobby features a wall with structural glazing.

Owner/Developer
Prime/Beitler Development Company LLC

Architect of Record
DeStefano + Partners

Design Consultant
Ricardo Bofill - Taller de Arquitectura

Structural Engineer
Thornton-Tomasetti Engineers

General Contractor
AMEC

Other Team Members

Mechanical, Electrical & Plumbing Engineer
Environmental Systems Design, Inc.
Civil Engineer
SDI Consultants Ltd.
Soils Consultant
STS Consultants, Inc.
Steel Fabricator
Kline Iron and Steel Co., Inc.
Steel Erector
American Bridge

Plaza 66, Shanghai

Plaza 66, the tallest concrete building in Shanghai, is a triumph of ingenuity over formidable obstacles. The tower is extremely slender (Fig.1), raising lateral stability issues. Local codes governing wind and seismic loads were stringent. The choice of building materials was limited. The site has a high water table and poor soils, and the tower is at the very edge of the property, compounding stability and foundation concerns. Kohn Pedersen Fox Associates, New York, designed the project, which also includes a five-story retail podium and three levels of underground parking.

The design team and the owner went to great lengths to overcome the constraints. James von Klemperer, KPF, says Thornton-Tomasetti played a major role in overcoming the biggest challenge, that of convincing local officials that their codes "could be seen in a different way." The engineers undertook a full-fledged effort, conducting extensive studies of buildings similar to Plaza 66. Their data, including wind tunnel test results that affirmed the performance and accelerations of the building under projected loads, convinced the local officials to waive some code provisions. The effort took "fortitude and stamina" by all parties, says von Klemperer.

1 A height-to-width ratio of nearly nine makes Shanghai's Plaza 66 exceptionally slender and posed challenges under the governing Chinese building codes. The effect is enhanced in this view by the tapered ends of the floor plan.

Before beginning structural design, Thornton-Tomasetti developed several structural systems, one entirely made of steel, one a composite, and one all concrete. When contractors estimated costs, the concrete design was the lowest by far. The material had other advantages: its damping properties and greater mass were appropriate for occupant comfort in the potentially windy city, and local contractors were familiar with concrete.

The tower's height and small footprint, 963 ft (294 m) high and between 74 ft (23 m) and 111 ft (34 m) wide, made outriggers essential. The engineers designed an innovative semi-rigid concrete outrigger system with openings for mechanical equipment and corridors on three tower levels (Figs.2,4). The two-story outriggers behave like Vierendeel trusses connecting the long face of the building core to the perimeter columns, resisting building overturning (Fig.3). The design team enlarged the exterior concrete columns at the tower base, from the basement parking levels up to the ground floor. This stiffens the columns enough to allow the use of semi-rigid outriggers. On upper floors, the column footprints are smaller, increasing rental space. The concrete columns and spandrel beams are rigidly connected to meet the local requirement for a special seismic moment frame providing stability and ductility.

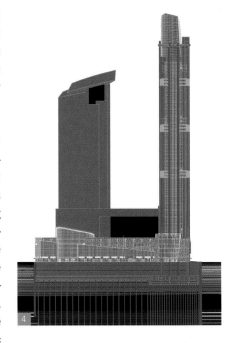

4 Outriggers at the three mechanical levels shown heavier at right in this diagram engage the full building width for overturning resistance. Foundations include piles of varying depths corresponding to the different loads under tower and podium areas.

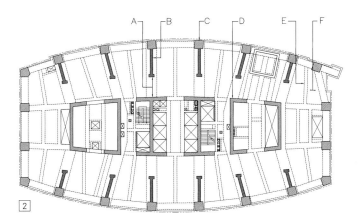

2 This mechanical room plan shows outriggers linking perimeter columns to the concrete core walls.
A Generous openings in outrigger walls accommodate mechanical equipment.
B Concrete shear wall of outrigger system.
C Perimeter column engaged by outrigger.
D Concrete core wall.
E Typical concrete floor beam; beam-and-slab framing occurs on all floors.
F Typical spanning direction for floor slabs.

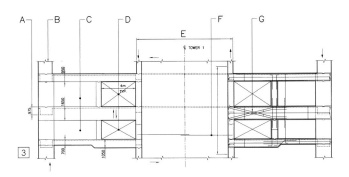

3 In this side view, outriggers in a two-story mechanical space engage three floor levels. Arrows show forces on the structure for wind coming from the right side.
A Typical perimeter beam for moment frame action.
B Perimeter column.
C Infill shear walls for outrigger action.
D Regular openings pass mechanical systems.
E Concrete core walls.
F Additional wall reinforcement for large forces at outrigger levels.
G Reinforcement bands in X pattern provide ductile shear resistance.

73

The foundation design was also executed in concrete. More than nine layers of compressible clay and sand underlie the site, and very different loads are applied by the tower and the podium. Thornton-Tomasetti designed a unique "honeycomb" concrete box mat that stiffens the basement for the tower with minimal weight (Fig.7). Concrete bored friction piles support the mat, delivering tower loads to lower strata efficiently.

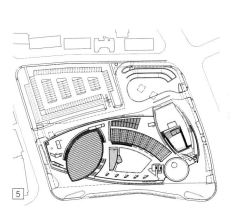

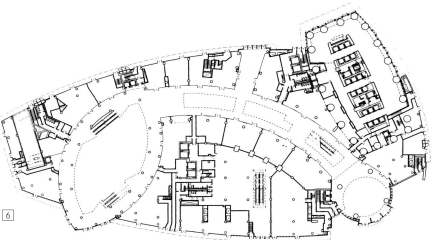

5,6 A large retail mall is housed within the podium to the left of the tower in this plan. The mall includes crescent- and lens-shaped atrium spaces.

7 This plan of the pile-supported tower foundation mat shows its cellular or "honeycomb" structure for stiffness with minimal weight. Also note the wall along the site boundary.
A Limit of tower foundation mat.
B Vertical web walls for the cellular foundation mat.
C Perimeter column rises from this point.
D Core wall outline is shown by dashed line.
E Tower perimeter above is shown by dashed line.
F Perimeter foundation wall cast in segments using the slurry wall method.
G Secant piles retain soil at temporary gaps in foundation wall to allow settlement.

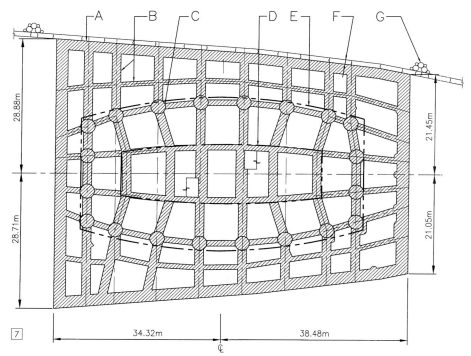

The site had a potential for significant settlement. To accommodate differing loads, the engineers left an unpoured zone in the mat. After initial settlement, the pour was completed. A seismic and thermal joint between the podium and the tower allows the two to behave independently above grade.

8 Mall atria roof planes are sloped relative to floors, creating a complex geometry.

Concrete figured in another economy. The podium with its complex layout was originally designed for steel, but concrete was used instead (Figs.5,6). It includes a large lens-shaped atrium skylight with deceptive geometry: the surface is flat, but not level. The glazed roof pitches both along the lens axis and perpendicular to it for dramatic effect (Fig.8). This required the supporting frames to follow complex shapes.

The engineers modified the structural design of these frames to use cast-in-place concrete in architectural forms for structural members (Figs.9,10,11).

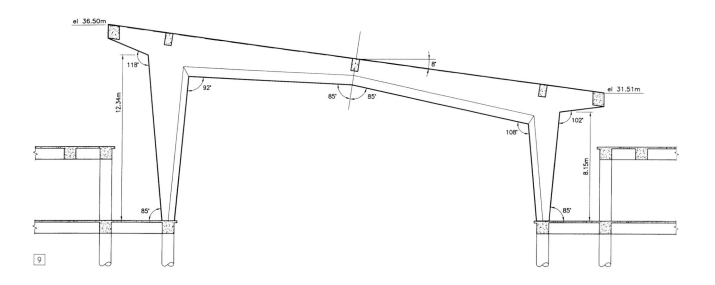

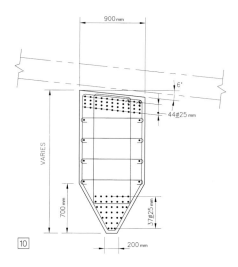

9 The crosswise slope of the atrium roof is not evident in the photo but is clearly shown in this frame elevation.

10 This section through a mall atrium roof frame shows its sculptural shape and heavy reinforcement, in addition to the roof pitch perpendicular to the rigid frames.

11 Sculpted concrete rigid frames span the atrium. While heavier than equivalent steel framing, this design takes full advantage of locally familiar and economical materials.

Plaza 66 is topped with a dramatic visor cantilevering 39 ft (12 m), and a 10-story glass lantern that also houses mechanical equipment and a three-story club room (Figs.12,13,14). Concrete would not have been a feasible construction material for that design and at that height, so it is carried on lightweight steel framing erected by hand using only a small crane (Fig.15). Lantern framing was then wrapped in translucent glass (Fig.16).

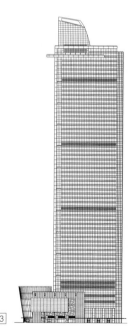

12 The tower top is enhanced by a dramatic cantilevered visor and a glass-enclosed ten-story-tall rooftop lantern.

13 Intentionally asymmetric podium and rooftop features enliven broad building faces of Plaza 66.

14 Glowing softly, the rooftop lantern creates a distinctive night-time signature on the Shanghai skyline.

Plaza 66 opened in 2001. The owner wanted a very tall building in a difficult location, and the design team fulfilled his expectations through ingenuity and extraordinary effort (Fig.17). It was "an adventurous, pioneering project," says architect von Klemperer.

Owner
Hang Lung Realty

Design Architect
Kohn Pedersen Fox Associates

Architect of Record
Frank CY Feng Architects

Structural Engineer
Thornton-Tomasetti Engineers

Owner's Representative
Hang Lung Project Management Ltd.

General Contractor
Shanghai Construction Group

Concrete Subcontractor
Shao Xin Construction Co.

Construction Manager
SCG #3 Construction

Other Team Members

Local Structural Engineer
East China Design Institute
Geotechnical Engineer
**Ho Tin and Associated Consulting
Engineers**
Mechanical, Electrical & Plumbing Engineer
Flack + Kurtz
Local Mechanical, Electrical & Plumbing
Associated Consulting Engineers

15 For construction convenience, steel framing supports the visor and lantern. Two planes of beams and columns are trussed together as horizontal rings and vertical frames, stabilized by shallow diagonal braces.

16 The presence of lantern steel framing can be detected through translucent glass that surrounds it, both inside and out.

17 The side elevation of Shanghai's Plaza 66 shows how mall atria, outrigger levels and the rooftop lantern are expressed.

79

Erie on the Park, Chicago

Erie on the Park in Chicago is a bold statement in steel. For this sleek 24-story residential tower, Lucien Lagrange Architects, Chicago, chose to emphasize the underlying structure with exposed chevron-shaped steel bracing punctuating the taut glass façade (Fig.2). The material and the design stand out in the Chicago cityscape, where exposed concrete is the typical choice for apartment buildings. Floor-to-ceiling glass spans between steel spandrels and the dramatic chevrons, achieving an open, airy look and offering building residents views of nearby Lake Michigan and the city skyline (Figs.2,3).

Architecture and structural engineering are virtually inseparable at Erie on the Park. The design team recognized several constraints: the owner wanted a wide variety of apartment layouts, 9 ft (2.7 m) ceilings for the units, and fast-track construction. Thornton-Tomasetti Engineers began by analyzing a concrete structural system, but were asked to look at an all-steel building due to the high cost of concrete frames at the time. Taking a cue from one of the most efficient steel buildings in Chicago – the

1 The strong geometry and exposed steel of Erie on the Park clearly distinguish it from surrounding concrete-framed apartment buildings.

2 The taut skin of Erie on the Park, a mix of horizontal glazing bands and architecturally exposed structural steel, is clearly visible in this view.

3 The site has great city views. Exterior bracing lines are continued above the rooftop as a celebration of their geometric strength.

John Hancock Center – a fully braced structure was explored. Timothy Hill of Lucien Lagrange explained that the exterior bracing approach evolved in a "very collaborative" process. Once Thornton-Tomasetti determined the type of bracing needed for the size and shape of the building, he says, their decision "influenced our esthetic expression (Fig.1)."

In one direction, the engineers placed bracing within two interior walls. In the perpendicular direction they developed the dramatic exterior chevron design, which derived from the angles determined for optimal bracing shapes (Fig.4).

The brace lines are linked to create a tube, effective in resisting the torsional wind loads acting on the eccentric form (Figs.6,7,8).

The bracing on each side forms eight vertically stacked chevrons 52 ft (15.9 m) wide; seven are three stories high, and the uppermost is two stories high. The building façade is an esthetic marriage of architectural interest and structural elegance. The diagonal elements transfer lateral loads from floor to floor, and a column bisects the chevrons for gravity resistance. (Fig.11) At the three-story-high lobby, construction transitions to concrete. (Fig.10) The base shear forces are transferred to concrete shear walls, and uplift is resisted by tension anchorages at the third level.

4 Architects and engineers collaborated to establish a bracing pattern that provides optimal structural behavior and appropriate visual impact. The result was a pattern of seven chevrons three stories high and one chevron two stories high.

5 The Xsteel program provided coordinated details and dimensions for smooth fabrication and erection of complex assemblies. This Xsteel rendering shows how exposed steel members and structural steel braces fit snugly together.

6 This Xsteel rendering shows the four lines of wind bracing, two along façades and two across the building. The four bracing lines are connected to form a torsionally stiff central spine, essential to resist twisting of the irregularly shaped floor plan.

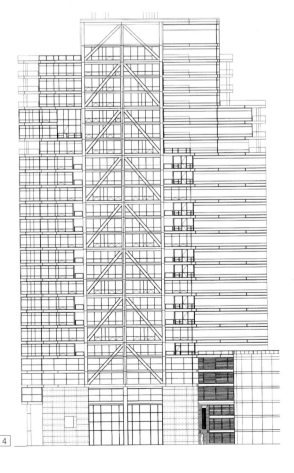

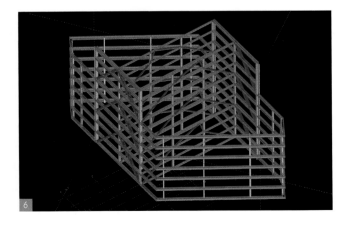

The interior floor system consists of steel wide-flange girders supporting 14 inch (356 mm) bar joists spaced 3 ft (0.9 m) apart, with 3/5 inch (15 mm) deep metal deck and 2 1/2 inches (63.5 mm) total concrete fill. The required fire rating is achieved by a combination of rated drywall ceilings and full sprinkler coverage. This system provided for easy erection and for routing of mechanical ducts and sprinklers within the 20 inch (508 mm) depth of the ceiling sandwich construction (Fig.9). It also allows for recessed lighting, another advantage for the owner and future tenants.

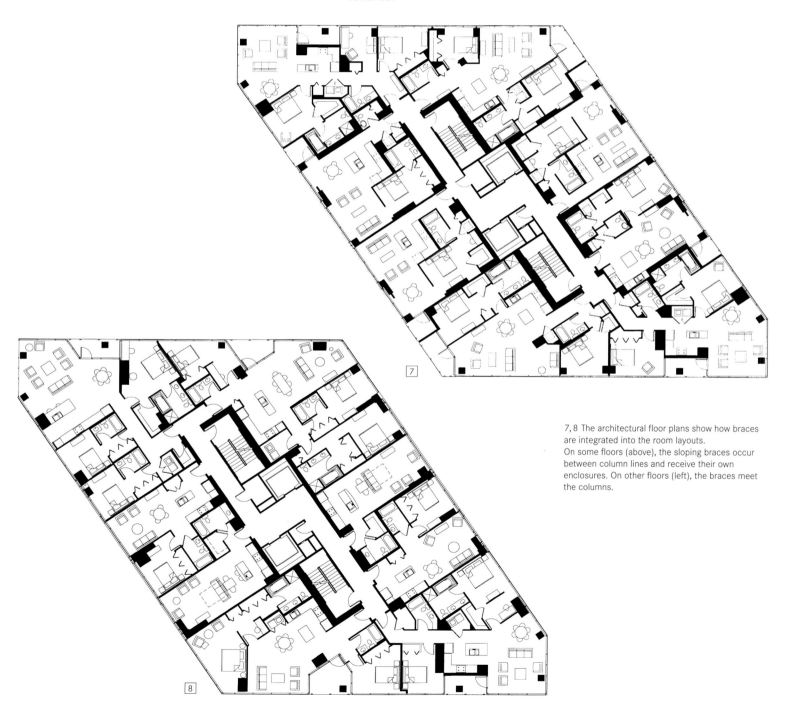

7, 8 The architectural floor plans show how braces are integrated into the room layouts.
On some floors (above), the sloping braces occur between column lines and receive their own enclosures. On other floors (left), the braces meet the columns.

The engineers created a 3-D Xsteel model of the steelwork on this project to accurately describe its difficult geometry. Xsteel allows geometry and member sizes to be exported to Computer Numerical Control (CNC) machines used in the steel fabrication industry. The geometric model of the structure was created in 3-D as well and transmitted to the steel fabricator to complete the connection details, also utilizing Xsteel. The result was a complex structural frame, including the cladding, that fit together smoothly during erection (Fig.5). The process contributed to the successful completion of this fast-track project. Erie on the Park opened in late 2002.

Owner/Developer
Smithfield Properties

Architect
Lucien Lagrange Architects

Structural Engineer
Thornton-Tomasetti Engineers

General Contractor
Wooton Construction

Other Team Members

Mechanical, Electrical & Plumbing Engineer
Advanced Mechanical Systems
Fire Protection Engineer
Global Fire Protection Company
Electrical Engineer
Innovative Building Concepts
Steel Fabricator
Zalk Josephs Fabricators
Steel Erector
Area Erectors
Steel Detailer
Dowco Consultants, Ltd.
Joist Fabricator
Canam Steel Corporation
Curtain Wall & Window Installation
Trainor Glass Company

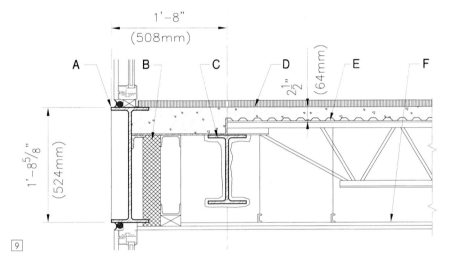

9

9 Typical floor construction includes:
A Architecturally exposed structural steel façade elements.
B Insulation behind the exposed steel.
C Structural steel girders with spray-on fireproofing.
D Concrete-filled metal deck floor slabs.
E Steel joists 14 inches (356 mm) deep, spaced every 3 ft (914 mm).
F Fire-rated ceiling construction meeting UL G501 to protect the steel joists.

10 The bottom three floors of project bracing transform to concrete shear walls to satisfy special requirements at the tall lobby. Steel framing is bolted to the top of the walls.

11 Each line of perimeter chevron braces is bisected by a gravity-load-bearing column, as is shown here.

Large Interior Spaces

The fundamental difference between the structure of projects in this chapter and the long-span structures described later is the architectural function of the framing. At an arena, the expectation is that all eyes will be on the players or performers. Long-span framing shapes and supports arena roofs, but is rarely featured inside the space. At these projects, in contrast, the structure is an important part of the architectural interior design. In several of the featured buildings, visible structure provides the esthetic expression and spatial organization.

Airline terminals have open, uncluttered floor space to allow free circulation of passengers, so the roof framing provides the architectural expression. At Terminal One in John F. Kennedy International Airport in New York, radially-oriented tied arches of steel perform three architectural functions: their spacing along the crescent-shaped airport terminal establishes a rhythm of narrow, tapering modules; their individual spans "leap" across portions of the cavernous concourse, and the combination of spans defines and supports the large curved roof profile. At United Airlines Terminal in Chicago's O'Hare International Airport, the repetitive steel frames that cross the concourses similarly establish a visually unifying rhythm, but also perform other functions. Intricate beam-to-column joints provide visual interest and permit a consistent column vocabulary using one to five clustered pipes. Asymmetrical frame shapes differentiate left and right in the long concourses, giving travelers a clear sense of direction. Varying frame heights provide a sense of location, as shorter frames denote concourse far ends. And different frame shapes in the two main concourses establish a unique identity for each.

Establishing unique identities was also the key concept for exposed structure in the lobbies of two intentionally similar Lucent Technologies Buildings near Chicago. Both buildings use glass and white-painted steel, so the different structural systems are essential design features that provide instantly recognizable landmarks. One lobby uses structural steel columns and wall bands to create a drum topped by a sloping dished roof reminiscent of a satellite dish. The other lobby welcomes visitors with steel trussed cantilever arms carrying a lower barrel-vaulted roof. A subtle linkage between the two buildings, a half mile apart, is the use of identical interior skylights that echo the barrel vault shape.

Although the materials are entirely different and the spans much shorter than in terminals, the Modern Art Museum of Fort Worth also uses structure to define interior space. Massive walls of highly finished, carefully detailed exposed concrete create distinctly different experiences within galleries protected from the intense Texas sun, and in the circulation spaces outside those walls but within the glass skin of each gallery module. Concrete roof girders of trapezoidal cross-section span the length of each building module, providing gallery layout flexibility and directing natural light that enters through clerestories and washes their sloping soffits. The gallery modules are visually terminated by giant concrete Y-shaped columns, signature features of the museum.

At some projects, the structure is the architecture. The features are proudly exposed, and the eye is not only attracted to the framing but is directed along it as the viewer intuitively understands the rational flow of forces. The World Financial Center Winter Garden in New York is such a space, where steel trussed arches span the gap between two office towers and support a fully glazed roof to create much-needed public space in a crowded downtown. The design developed from an esthetic of structural efficiency. For such projects, architectural ideas spring from load path requirements, and clever structural solutions take advantage of architectural features, such as the use of offset planes in a huge end wall to create an inconspicuous truss.

In other buildings with large spaces, structure may be even less visible. The UBS Investment Bank exemplifies the push and pull between architectural and engineering design depending on the structure's end use. This building has a dramatic long-span roof, but the open span is required to create a column-free trading floor. The interior work space is hardly bare-bones or oppressive. The roof design is bright and even lyrical. The structural framing system selected to support the roof is visible; but through integration with the architectural ceiling treatment it is unobtrusive. Its engineering also incorporates an innovative construction system consisting of compressed mid-span posts and pretensioned bottom chord cables to resist roof uplift.

Other projects have interior spaces that rely on elaborate structural framing without necessarily exposing it. The Overture Center for the Arts in Madison, Wisconsin, includes extensive retrofits of existing structural systems to incorporate old theater spaces into a complex with new uses of interior space, including a concert hall with sensitive acoustic requirements. The engineers successfully employed cantilevers, transfer trusses, and special connections for acoustic isolation throughout the site to provide an economical and acoustically appropriate structural design solution.

These projects illustrate the great variety of structural solutions available to work with the architecture of large interior spaces. Structure can be featured for visual identity and organization at airport terminals, gathering spaces and signature lobbies, or it can be expressed unobtrusively as part of a trading hall ceiling. Structural elements can mold space and light in a museum, or work "behind the scenes" to make complex performance centers practical. The common element for all these situations is extensive collaboration between architectural and structural designers that results in solutions that best meet user needs.

UBS Investment Bank, Stamford

Not every long-span structure is an arena or airport terminal. Trading floors for financial institutions also require large column-free spaces, and bring their own design challenges. When UBS Investment Bank (at that time, Swiss Bank) decided to put their U.S. operations under one roof, they chose Skidmore, Owings & Merrill (SOM), Chicago, as the architect. The Stamford, Connecticut, project features the world's largest clear-span trading floor, currently 144 ft (43.9 m) by 360 ft (109.7 m). The bank complex also includes an office tower, a five-story parking garage and a five-story glass-enclosed lobby with a dramatic suspended staircase that hugs the interior wall (Fig.3).

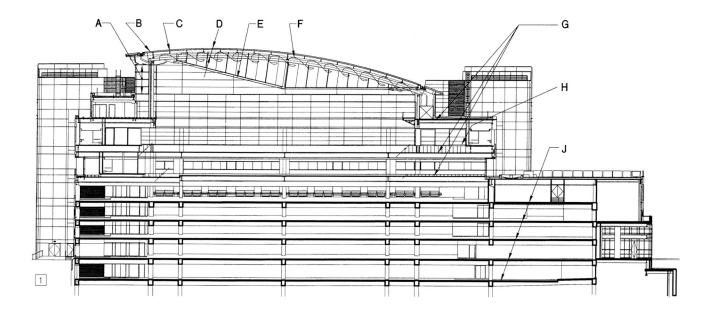

1 Sufficient height for a clerestory window was created by canting the roof over the trading floor. This cross-section shows key elements of the long-span portion of the project.
A Clerestory window height.
B Roof decking.
C Structural steel purlins, W16 (400 mm deep).
D Curving top chords of boxes fabricated from steel plate.
E Twin-cable bottom chords.
F "Wave" ceiling panels.
G Steel-framed floor and roof construction.
H Raised flooring for wiring; note especially large space at trading floor level.
J Cast-in-place, post-tensioned, concrete-framed floors at parking levels below the trading floor.

Mustafa Abadan, SOM's senior designer for the headquarters building, says that "structural support was an integral part of the architecture." In close collaboration with Thornton-Tomasetti Engineers, the design team explored more than ten structural options. Their goal was to provide a large column-free space with a strong esthetic statement that would also be economical to construct. The design that emerged has a canted roof to create a clerestory space that admits natural light (Figs.1,2). The long spans are carried by nine king-post trusses with arched top chords. Each truss works like a bow and arrow: the bottom tension chord "string" of twin steel

2 This drawing looking outward at the clerestory wall shows the X-braced framing system and the extent of clerestory windows. The legend for the cross-section applies here as well.

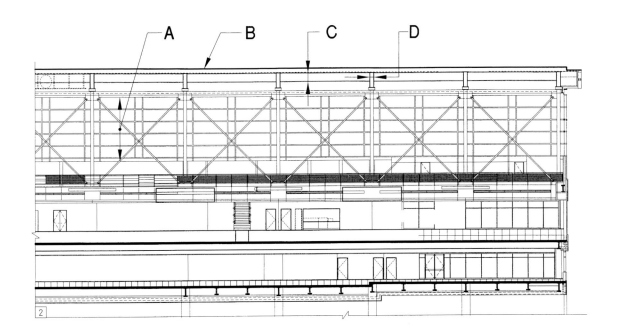

3 The UBS Investment Bank project includes office space and parking levels, capped by a long-span trading floor with its curved-chord king-post truss roof framing expressed on the exterior.

cables pushes up against a 16 ft (4.9 m) long king-post "arrow," while the top chord "bow," a 144 ft (43.9 m) curved steel box girder, acts in compression and flexure (Fig.5). The bottom chord was pretensioned, so it does not go slack even in wind uplift conditions. The resulting system is stiff, efficient, and visually unobtrusive (Fig.4).

Because the structural system is totally visible, the esthetics were critical. SOM mandated that the tension chords be unencumbered by the bulky mechanical connections, such as turnbuckles, that are often used for cable tensioning or adjustment (Fig.9). To add to the construction challenge, the architect required that the completed trusses have rooftop and king-post elevations that line up perfectly, within a 3 inch (76 mm) tolerance.

4 The twin bottom chords in tension push upward on the pipe post at mid-span to support the box top chord of these roof trusses. Joint detailing was made both clean and practical to fabricate.

5 By using thin bottom chord members, pretensioned to permit tension-only design even in the event of uplift, the roof framing of this long-span column-free trading floor is visually unobtrusive.

The contractor, the erection engineer, on-site staff and Thornton-Tomasetti all helped to devise an elegant scheme that met SOM's dimensional requirements while also satisfying structural pretensioning requirements. The truss elements were fabricated to exact length, including tension chords shop-fabricated precisely using prestretched cables. In the field, arched top chords were set on temporary shores with slack cables and king posts "telescoped" short on internal sleeves (Figs.6,7,8). A temporary frame then provided "archery" action: a small jack simultaneously pushed the top chord upward, pulled the bottom cables downward and stretched the telescoped king-post about 24 inches (610 mm) (Fig.10). Once jack force and truss geometry both met design criteria, split-pipe segments were field-cut and welded to fix the king-post at its final length.

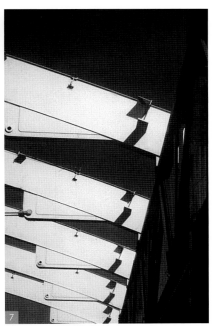

6 With top chord, bottom cables and king post assembled, pretensioning of the trusses was ready to proceed.

7 Truss ends use simple gusset plates aligned with box chord faces to receive the tension chord clevises.

8 Truss top chords were fabricated, shipped and erected in half-span lengths, bearing on temporary shores. The chord halves were joined by field-welding. Then bottom chord cables, prefabricated to exact length, were installed slack.

9 The "bow and arrow" nature of the roof construction is clear from this isometric drawing. Also note the visually unobtrusive connections at truss mid-span and ends, and the X-braced clerestory wall using alternating single and paired rods to pass each other cleanly.

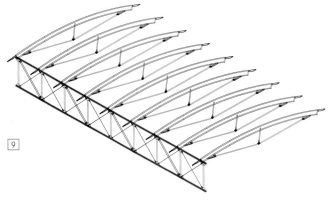

The ceiling for the trading space includes mechanical, acoustical and lighting systems within a dramatic series of waves, following the building's subtle nautical theme. Suspension of the monumental staircase in the glassed-in lobby uses that theme as well (Figs.11,12). SOM's Mustafa Abadan credits Thornton-Tomasetti for the "esthetically pleasing, almost invisible cable connection, inspired by sailboat design." Steven Weinryb, SOM's senior technical coordinator for the bank project, cites Thornton-Tomasetti's flexibility, saying that the firm "looks at design problems with a new perspective."

10 This clever device "drew the arrow" of the center post to pretension the bottom chords and flex the top chord to proper force and elevation. The center post was fabricated short, and a narrower pipe "telescopes" inside it at the top. A small jack, visible just above the bottom of the temporary frame, simultaneously pulled down on the post lower end and up on the top chord, "stretching" the "telescoped" vertical post. Jack force, cable tension and chord elevation were all compared and, when correct, half-pipes were cut to length to cover the post gap and welded into place. The "arrow" was permanently "drawn."

The UBS Investment Bank opened in 1997 with a temporary wall along the east edge of the garage, data and trading floors. The wall was removed for a phase two expansion, completed in 2002. The trading floor was extended by 120 ft (36.6 m) through the addition of four more trusses, and the garage now has four more parking bays. Planned future phases will include additional office towers in spaces adjacent to the current development.

Owner
UBS Investment Bank

Developer
Hines

Architect
Skidmore, Owings & Merrill, LLP

Structural Engineer
Thornton-Tomasetti Engineers

General Contractor
Turner Construction Co.

Owner's Representative
Hines Interests LP

Other Team Members

Mechanical, Electrical & Plumbing/Lighting Engineer
Cosentini Associates
Civil / Traffic Engineer
Allan Davis Associates
Geotechnical Engineer
Langan Engineering and Environmental Services
Acoustical Consultant
Cerami and Associates
Elevator Consultant
Van Deusen & Associates
Information Technology
Schiff & Associates
Kitchen Consultant
Cini Little International
Landscape Architect
Weintraub + di Domenico
Environmental Engineer
Metcalf & Eddy

11,12 A monumental stair through the main lobby expresses a nautical theme through its suspension system: sailboat-style hardware and rigging cables.

Terminal One,
John F. Kennedy International Airport, New York

Terminal One at John F. Kennedy International Airport opened in 1999 and became house to four airlines: JAL, Lufthansa, Korean Air, and Air France. For this new terminal, architect William Nicholas Bodouva and Associates, New York, designed a building that challenges the visual senses. The engineers responded to the architect's concept with a practical solution that visually leaps across space and balances inherent eccentric loads. The bare bones of the structural system are a rib cage of radial arches that span the building, and curved triangular truss "spines" that intersect the arches and form support lines.

Architect Bodouva says of the design effort, "Thornton-Tomasetti Engineers proved innovative and supportive of the designer's vision, and the team emerged with a structural concept that confronts the lyrical and the romantic. With their help early in the process, we created a building that is functional, rational, and imaginative."

The building envelope is complex. The terminal roof is a sector of a torus – a 45 degree slice in plan from an imaginary donut with a center point far outside the entrance. A flat north front wall cuts across the inside of the donut hole; its intersection with the downward-sloping roof varies in height, creating a "smile-shaped" surface high above the terminal entrance (Fig.2). A glazed roof over the first bay creates an inviting entry, and the sidewalk canopy cantilevers from the front wall with no apparent backup (Fig.5). The rear wall follows the outer curve of the torus. The end

2 The roof of Terminal One is based on a torus or donut. The intersection of that surface with the flat entry wall creates a distinctive "smile." Glass walls let daylight pour through the building.

1 Each end wall dramatically leans out above a skewed fold line.

walls are glass, each with a fold on a skewed line from the ground to the roof. Below that line the walls are vertical; above they lean out as much as 18 ft (5.5 m) (Fig.1).

The structural framing allows for ample interior circulation space with no typical column layouts, bay sizes or curtain walls (Fig.4). The 26 tied arches offer visual rhythm through their "leaping" radial pattern (Figs.3,8,9,10). Concrete

3 Radial arches create a strong rhythm throughout the terminal.

4 Radial building geometry is clearly shown by the roof framing plan. Radial arch designs vary with building depth as shown by section marks. Note ten widely spaced columns along line 2, and the following features:
A Glazed roof at entry.
B Roof bracing for lateral loads.
C Tri-chord truss spanning to columns.

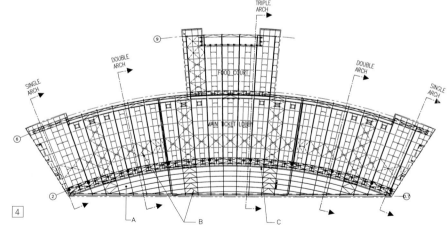

columns spaced along an arc through the middle of the terminal catch every third radial line. Continuous triangular pipe trusses, curved to align with the columns, support the other arches (Figs.6,7).

The design of Terminal One involved complicated loads. The cantilevers and variable spans generate horizontal loads under self-weight; the folded cantilevered side walls also require horizontal restraint to stand under

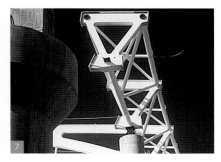

5 A skylit first bay creates an inviting entry to the terminal and starts the pattern of "leaping" tied arches that cross the building.

6 The terminal's main structural spine is a steel triangular truss that carries radial arches and spans to stiff concrete columns.

7 The triangular truss "spine" was erected ahead of the radial tied arches.

8 Single arch.

9 Double arch.

10 Triple arch. Radial tied arch designs follow the same pattern, but vary depending on loading conditions.
Key elements are as follows:
A Rear steel tri-chord truss.
B W36 (900 mm deep) steel column.
C W24 (600 mm deep) steel roof girder, tilted.
D W16 (400 mm deep) steel purlin, cambered.
E 3-4 inch (76-101 mm) diameter steel pipes used as tension ties.
F 6 inch (152 mm) steel pipe hangers.
G Tri-chord steel truss central spine.
H 60 inch (1524 mm) diameter concrete column.
J Laterally guided vertical slip connection.
K Building face.
L 2-4 inch (50-101 mm) diameter steel pipe tension ties.
M 12 inch (305 mm) diameter steel pipe purlins.
N Sloping steel planar truss.
P Entry canopy steel-framed cantilever.
Q W24 (600 mm deep) steel column.

gravity; and wind loads on the walls and seismic forces on the roof create additional lateral loads. All these forces are carried down through the open space by vertical bracing concealed along the rear wall and cantilever column stiffness elsewhere. The roof acts as a diaphragm to collect these forces and distribute them to the points of restraint.

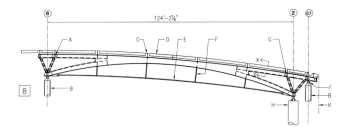

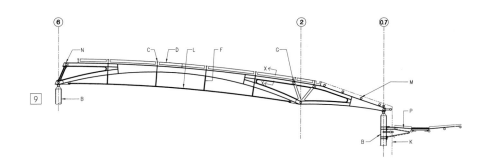

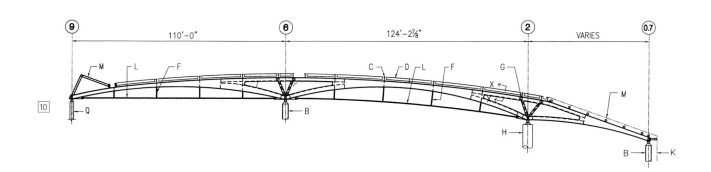

The side walls' fold is defined by vertical boomerang trusses that resist only wind pressure and glazing self-weight (Figs.11,12). The New York City fire code does not mandate fireproofing for non-load-bearing elements, so the structural scheme for these walls retained the architect's vision and avoids the costs of fireproofing and cladding. Only lateral loads are transmitted to roof framing, through a special slip joint.

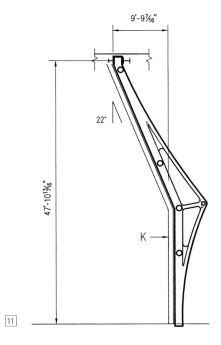

11 This folded-wall truss occurs at section WW in the end wall framing elevation. The overhang varies along the wall, but the 22 degree slope is constant. A sliding detail at the upper tip of the truss restrains lateral forces but allows free vertical motion, so the truss is not classified as "load-bearing."

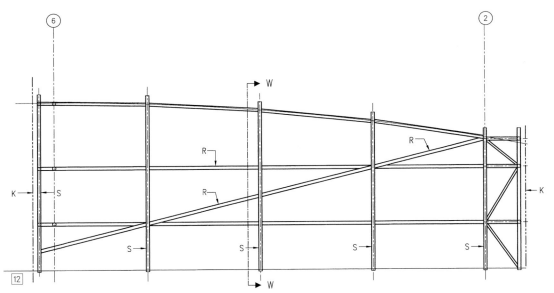

12 This end wall framing elevation shows the diagonal member that defines the folded glazing and the end truss that helps hold its shape. Section WW refers to the bent truss in the adjacent drawing.
K Building face.
R 12 inch (304 mm) diameter steel pipe girt.
S Folded-wall steel truss.

The structural engineers realized economies in several ways. The arches were fabricated from plates that were analyzed for buckling and tested for weld distortion to find the thinnest possible steel (Fig.13). The plates were joined using fillet welds, less labor-intensive than other types. Long arch spans came to the site in two half-spans; splices were field-welded and tie rods were installed on the ground for better quality control (Fig.14).

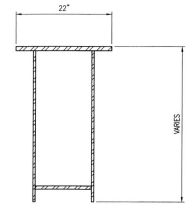

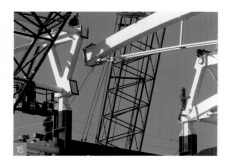

The arches were then lifted into place and connected to the transverse, triangulated pipe trusses (Figs.17,18). To simplify and speed erection, those connections were unobtrusive bolted end plates, rather than time-consuming field welds (Figs.15,16). Terminal One shows how highly complex spatial geometries can be created, visualized and analyzed, using 3-D computer-aided design, and then made a reality.

Owner/Developer
Terminal One Group Association

Architect
William Nicholas Bodouva

Structural Engineer
Thornton-Tomasetti Engineers

General Contractor
AMEC

Project Manager
Parsons Brinkerhoff Construction Services, Inc.

Other Team Members

Mechanical, Electrical & Plumbing Engineer
Joseph R. Loring
Site/Civil Engineer
The STV Group and Associates
Steel Subcontractor
Canron Construction Corp.
Concrete & Pile Subcontractor
Century Maxim & Pile Foundations
Curtain Wall Fabricator/Erector
Flour City Architectural Metals, Inc.

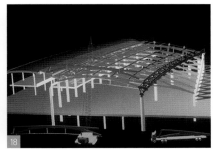

13 At the sections marked XX on the arch drawings, (See Figs.8-10) a "pi"(π)-shaped box section is provided. Steel plates are joined using simple, economical fillet welds (not shown here).

14 For each span, arch halves were shipped prefabricated to the site, where they were joined, and tie rods were installed on the ground. These tied arches are waiting for erection.

15 To speed erection, arch-to-truss joints use simple bolted end plate connections. Detailing and fabrication considered erection clearances and fit-up tolerances.

16 The completed arch-to-truss connections are inconspicuous and architecturally acceptable.

17 Each arch is connected to the central triangular trussed spine, one side at a time.

18 Each color in this diagram indicates a different type of erection piece: triangle trusses, single-span arches and each bay of multiple-span arches.

Modern Art Museum, Fort Worth

Tadao Ando's new Modern Art Museum of Fort Worth, Texas, is a celebration of concrete. Ando brings the material to new heights of elegance, while paying homage to Louis I. Kahn, concrete's early architectural advocate. The Kimbell Museum, designed by Kahn almost 40 years ago, sits opposite Ando's 21st-century creation.

1 The design of the Modern Art Museum of Fort Worth is based on a "box in a box" – a glass curtain wall wrapping around concrete walls with high quality finish. At night, lights washing the inner, concrete walls spill out through the glazed envelope and reflect off the surrounding pond, creating an effect of floating Japanese lanterns.

2 Dramatic overhangs, propped by Y-columns, shade the five modules making up the museum.

When Ando won the competition to design the new museum, his passion for exquisitely finished cast-in-place concrete raised structural engineering and construction issues rare in U.S. practice. The main problem was posed by the complex roof design. To realize Ando's conception, Thornton-Tomasetti Engineers, architects Kendall/Heaton Associates, contractor Linbeck Construction, a concrete consultant and others worked closely in the design process. Architect Rollie Childers of Kendall/Heaton called it "continuous collaboration."

The museum is a "box within a box." A glass curtain wall envelops five galleries, alternately double- and single-storied, a café, offices and circulation areas (Figs.1,2). The complex roof has two levels to diffuse light throughout the interior without exposing paintings to ultraviolet rays. Five independent, parallel strips form the high roof that spans the museum. Daylight passing between the strips reflects off lower roof panels and high roof soffits, entering the galleries through clerestories (Figs.3,4).

3 This building partial cross-section drawing, cut through alternating 24 and 40 ft. (7.3 and 12.2 m) wide galleries, shows the complex roof system used to control lighting conditions.
A Capping the concrete folded plate roof with an upper slab creates torsionally stiff roof strips that are stabilized only at their ends.
B Skylight between high roof strips.
C Light-diffusing ceiling under each skylight.
D Sunshade trellises project from roof strips over the wider galleries.
E Suspended post-tensioned concrete low roof panel.
F Expansion joint between structural mullion and roof to keep mullions thin.
G Overhang to shade glazed envelope from the Texas sun.
H Hangers support the suspended low roof; clerestory windows run between hangers.
J Ductwork fits in the space between low roof and gallery ceiling.
K Exposed, high-finish concrete wall "inner box."
L Structural mullion resists wind load on glazing by fixed base and propped top connections.
M Glazed outer building envelope.
N Second-floor slab of cast-in-place concrete.
P First-floor slab of cast-in-place concrete.
Q Basement level.

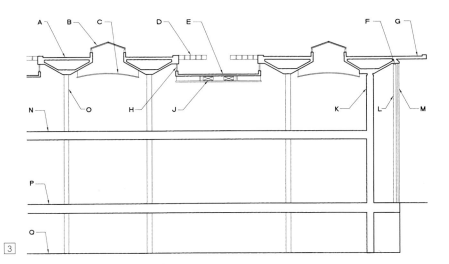

Thin-edged roof overhangs provide shelter from the Texas sun and bear on five 40 ft (12.2 m) high Y-shaped columns (Fig.5). While the finish of the exposed concrete was a major issue, the structural engineering was equally critical: "The Y-columns and the high roof sections are where the structure is most visible, and where the structural engineering defines the architecture," says Childers.

Thornton-Tomasetti studied 20 schemes for the high roof, focusing on fold-ed-plate systems. In early schemes, crossbeams held the folded shape and resisted tipping. Then the engineers found that adding a slab over the central trough in each roof created a torsionally stiff spine (Fig.6) that eliminated the need for crossbeams and simplified drainage. The modifica-tion improved esthetics and enhanced the natural light in the galleries. The final roof design used continuous, cast-in-place concrete.

4 Sunshine reflected through the clerestory louvers washes gallery ceilings and walls with natural light. Note shallow construction of the suspended lower roof slab.

5 Thin projecting roof slab edges are supported by Y-columns standing outside the glass envelope. Their visibility made proper finish on the Y-columns a critical consideration, leading to special construction methods. The café ellipse beyond appears to knife into the building.

Integrating mechanical distribution space with the ceiling heights and walls of Ando's concept took months. Thornton-Tomasetti and the design team created space for the second floor ceiling plenum by using very thin, flat, post-tensioned slabs for the lower roof. The slabs, only 6.5 inches (165 mm) thick, form hanging panels with upturned edges that provide a sill for the clerestories (Fig.7).

The engineers also used slab post-tensioning to eliminate some stiffening beams in the high roof overhang above the Y-columns. The result is a cleaner exterior roofline. In another team effort, the number of continuous architectural concrete walls in the original gallery design was reduced to those locations necessary for stability and load resistance, and where esthetically desirable. The change provided more flexibility for hanging art; only the ends of the galleries, visible through the glass curtain wall, are continuous high-finish architectural concrete.

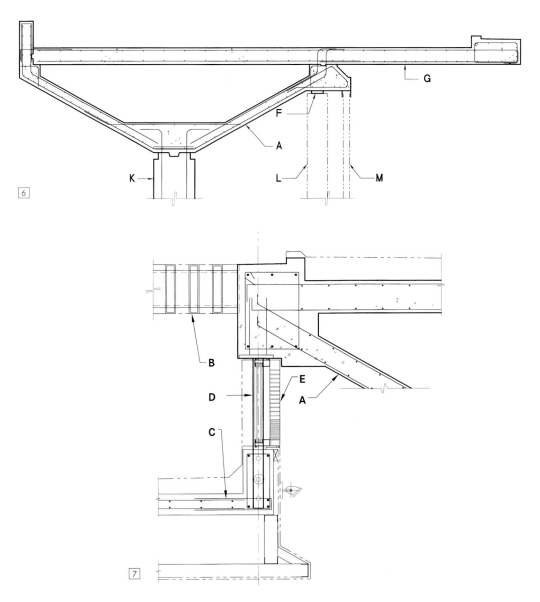

6 A two-pour construction scheme made roof elements torsionally stiff box beams, capable of resisting unbalanced loads such as the overhang shown here.
A Upper roof box section.
F Vertical slip joint.
G Overhang slab.
K Inner concrete.
L Outer wall mullion.
M Outer wall glazing.

7 Light enters the wider galleries after passing through sun shades and bouncing off the low roof and the sloping soffit of the upper roof box.
A Upper roof box section.
B Sun shading trellis.
C Suspended lower roof panel.
D Hanger and clerestory glazing.
E Interior sun control.

The Y-columns posed another concrete quandary. Ando wanted these key architectural statements to be cast in place, but the concrete vibrators would have damaged forms for the sloping arms, marring the finish. Thornton-Tomasetti and the contractor devised an ingenious method to cast column pieces vertically on site, then lift them into place with connections embedded at the column reveal (Figs.8-11 and 12-15).

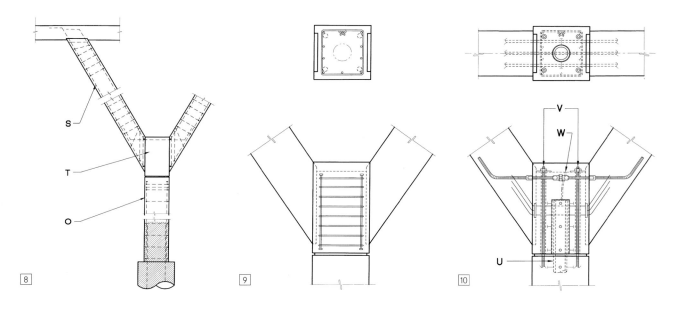

8 Elements of the Y-column, shown carrying the roof slab.
O Lower column, cast in its final position.
S Upper arm segment, cast in separate formwork in a vertical position.
T Joint between upper arm segments, cast to link upper arms.

9 The cast-in-place concrete joint linking upper arms contains its own cage of reinforcing bars. Note that arms protrude into the joint.

10 In addition to reinforcement, the Y-column joint contains complex hardware to hold the upper arms in alignment prior to casting, and permit fastening to the lower column. Note the reveal just below the upper arms. It matches reveals elsewhere in the building and helps conceal the field joint at this location.

U The central spine is cast into the lower column, and a mating pocket is cast into the joint.
V Hold-down bolts in four corners keep the upper arms in position until final grouting.
W Grout tube projects up from the central spine. Once grouting is complete, the tubes are removed and the top pocket is filled flush.

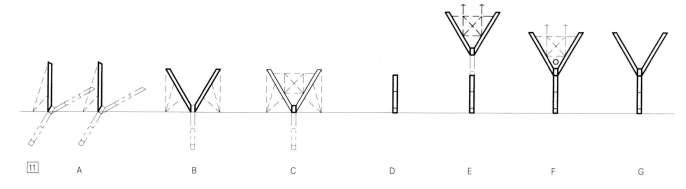

11 Careful segmental construction was used to assure excellent concrete finish.
A Two upper arm segments are cast in formwork held vertically.
B Upper arms are set in alignment using a cradle.

C Central joint is cast between upper arms.
D Building column is cast nearby.
E Upper arms and central joint are lifted atop the column.

F The central joint is connected to the column by bolting and by grouting to a center spine.
G The Y-column is complete and ready to receive roof slab concrete.

The museum's café posed yet another critical engineering puzzle. Its elliptical concrete roof, with one sector "knifed" into the main building, was to stand with minimal support: a quarter-circle wall, a main building wall and two columns (Figs.17,18). To minimize undesirable wall forces, Thornton-Tomasetti designed the post-tensioned roof to deflect under initial self-weight while bearing on just two columns (Fig.16).

12 The mating surface under the upper joint shows provisions for bolts, for the central spine, and for several shear keys.

13 An exact fit was essential for high-quality results.

14 Here upper arms have been joined, and the whole upper assembly is being lifted for placement on the lower column. Lowering the upper assembly was done carefully to clear bolts and spine.

15 The completed Y-column, ready for roof construction to proceed overhead.

16 Post-tensioning strands in the roof slab of the café structure direct most of its weight onto just a few columns like the one seen here.

17 For the café roof, this reinforcing bar arrangement may look simple, but making a thick, tapering, elliptical slab appear to float is not.

18 The café roof appears to knife into the main building. But actually the connections from the café roof to the main building were made after loads were in place. They primarily aid roof stability.

105

Once equilibrium was reached after formwork removal, grout was pumped in pre-placed sleeves to complete the wall connections. The project also includes a cast-in-place post-tensioned concrete bridge crossing the main lobby. Such bridges are often featured in Ando designs (Figs.19-24).

As one of Tadao Ando's few buildings in the U.S., the Modern Art Museum of Fort Worth sets new standards for architectural concrete in this country, as well as for design. The museum opened in December 2002.

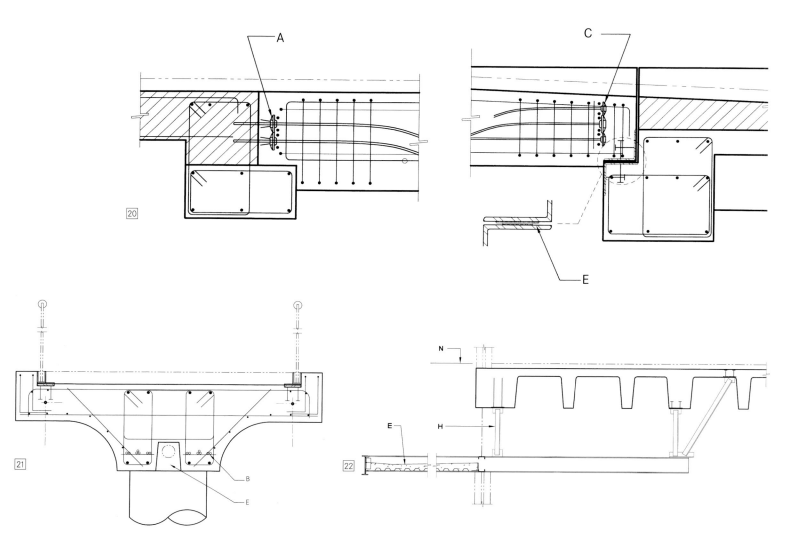

19 A concrete bridge linking second-floor galleries and offices appears shallow and light due to continuous coves and use of post-tensioned construction.

20 Enlarged ends of the bridge side view.
(See Fig.23)
A Jacking location for the post-tensioning strand. Concrete shown hatched was cast after jacking.
C "Dead end" of the strand.
E Detail of the slide bearing provided at the right end.

21 Cross-section showing the cove detail used along the lobby bridge soffit.
B Post-tensioning strand, elevation varies.
E Continuous groove for sprinkler system (dashed), running full length of bridge and through column tops.

22 Suspended steel canopy framing and typical pan system of concrete floor framing.
E Canopy concrete fill on deck pitched to drain.
H Steel hanger connected to embedded plates.
N Elevation of finished floor slab.

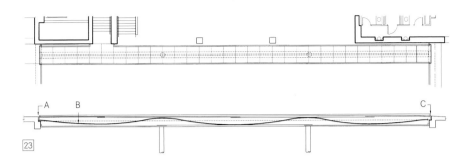

23

23 This plan (above) and side view (below) shows the lobby bridge layout, with post-tensioning strand and concrete walls shown bold.
A Fixed end of the bridge and active end of the strand.
B Profile of the post-tensioning strand.
C Expansion joint for the bridge, and inactive end of the strand.

24 The soaring lobby is crossed by a concrete bridge linking wings at the second floor.

Owner
MPA Foundation

Design Architect
Tadao Ando Architect & Associates

Architect of Record
Kendall/Heaton Associates, Inc.

Structural Engineer
Thornton-Tomasetti Engineers

Consulting Architect
Richard Fitzgerald & Associates

Landscape Architect
SWA Group

Owner's Representative
Peter Edward Arendt, AIA

General Contractor
Linbeck Construction Co.

Other Team Members

Mechanical, Electrical & Plumbing Engineer
CHPA Consulting Engineers
Civil Engineer
Huitt–Zollars Inc.
Curtain Wall Consultant
Peter M. Muller, Inc.

24

United Airlines Terminal
at O'Hare International Airport, Chicago

The United Airlines Terminal at Chicago O'Hare International Airport is a splendid example of expressed architecture. With an exposed structural skeleton reminiscent of a grand 19th-century train depot, this marriage of structural engineering and the architecture of Murphy/Jahn Architects, Chicago, achieves real distinction in a rhythmic design with exquisite steel details.

The terminal is composed of four main public spaces: a column-free 810 by 120 ft (246.9 by 36.6 m) ticketing area, the adjacent 1,700 ft (518.2 m) long Concourse B, a slightly shorter Concourse C, and a connecting tunnel below an airport taxiway (Fig.1). The 300,000 square foot (27,871 square meter) pedestrian tunnel makes transfers between concourses a lively experience, with moving walkways, background music and ever-changing kaleidoscopic neon on the ceiling, but daylight enlivens the other spaces.

1 This aerial view of United Airlines Terminal at O'Hare International Airport in Chicago shows 1700 ft (518.2 m) long Concourse B with one curved end in the foreground, a ticketing area with a folded-plate roof by its side, and Concourse C beyond the parked aircraft, linked by a passageway under the taxiway.

Concourses B and C are barrel vaults topped by clear and fritted glass, carefully arranged to control sunlight throughout the day (Fig.3). Their architecture is defined by the rhythm of transverse closely-spaced white-painted steel frames passing overhead. The Concourse B vault stands 40 ft (12.2 m) tall, then steps down to 30 ft (9.1 m) before terminating as a half-dome. Concourse C has a different frame profile and steps from 30 to 20 ft (9.1 to 6.1 m) in height along its length (Fig.2). The frames were three-plate weldments, with a web cut to the desired curve and flanges fitted to follow.

2 The Concourse C vault has its own distinctive profile. A step between high and low vaults can be seen in the distance.

3 A mixture of clear glass, fritted glass and solid panels controls daylight within the high vaults of Concourse B.

The exposed structural components provide a consistent design vocabulary throughout the terminal. Concourse glass mullions mount to purlins running longitudinally. The tubular steel pipe purlins link transverse frames together for lateral stability, deliver horizontal loads to X-bracing bands that periodically wrap the building, participate in the X-brace system, and bend to wrap around the half-domes at concourse ends (Fig.5).

The purlins bolt to the top flanges of transverse steel frames created by shop-welding pre-bent flange plates to a web cut from plate to follow the desired vault curve. Each main frame web also sports a series of shop-cut holes to create the feeling of aircraft framing and transmit light, reducing the visual "heft" of the steel (Fig.4). Even where frame shapes differ, consistent frame proportions and web openings create a unified design.

Another unifying feature is the treatment of columns. While loads on individual columns vary widely, all are variations on a theme: clustered steel pipes, 8 5/8 inches (219 mm) in diameter, joined together with frequent batten plates to form a rigid unit.

4 The visual lightening effect of frame web perforations is evident on this Concourse C low vault frame during construction. Vault frames are three-plate weldments following a web cut to the desired curved shape.

5 Concourse vault terminations use horizontal purlins as primary members, wrapping around a half-dome shape. Purlin and glazing weight is suspended from the last frame by radial 1 7/8 inch (48 mm) diameter sag rods.

Much like the five column orders of classical architecture, there are five variations in the United Airlines Terminal, consisting of columns made of one, two, three, four or five pipes. Typical concourse frames join to three-pipe columns by embedment within the column tops and termination at a 45 degree end cut (Fig.7).

Column battens have central holes that echo the frame webs, and the skewed frame end passes through the center of the top batten hole – a steel fabrication challenge successfully met throughout the project. The architectural intent of this intricate detail was an impression that the roof weight "floats" above the columns. Four-pipe columns occur between Concourse B and the ticketing area (Fig.8) and where frames cross columns (Fig.9).

Five-pipe columns carry paired concourse frames at vault roof steps, and single-pipe columns support short-span frames at gate lounges and the connecting link to other O'Hare terminals (Fig.6). All the supported frames repeat the 45 degree end cut detail.

6 A connector to other terminals maintains the design vocabulary of curved wide-flange vault frames, perforated webs and 45 degree terminations sliced into single-pipe columns.

7 Three-pipe columns typically occur along concourse sides. Roof vault frames knife through column top plates and terminate on a 45 degree skew cut that passes through the center of the top batten hole. The architectural goal was an impression of vault frames floating free of the columns. Precision fabrication was required for a consistent appearance across hundreds of such connections.

8 At these four-pipe columns under construction, Concourse B frames knife between the left pair of pipes, while ticketing hall folded-plate trusses land on the right pair.

9 Where columns are crossed by horizontal vault frames, a four-pipe configuration maintains the floating appearance.

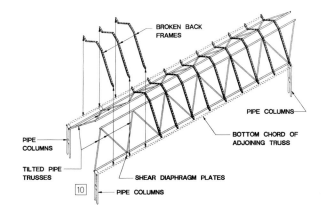

Two-pipe columns support the front of the ticketing hall (Fig.11). Providing the structural system for this huge column-free space was the greatest engineering demand of the project. Thornton-Tomasetti Engineers' solution was elegant and economical. They designed a structural system that was easily shipped and erected, a folded plate roof composed of tilted steel pipe trusses that lean against each other in pairs, with gaps topped by narrow skylights that admit filtered light (Fig.12).

There are 27 sets of paired trusses, each 30 ft (9.1 m) wide. Truss pairs would have been too long and wide to truck to the site assembled, but individual flat trusses were shallow enough to ship as half-length pieces. Four single-plane half-length trusses were assembled on a rolling jig parked in a distant area of the airport. Once truss splices were welded and truss pairs were bolted together, the jig was driven to the building site. Each pair resisted erection forces and formed a stable unit (Fig.10). The trusses were also light for easy lifting and economical shipping.

10 The folded-plate ticketing roof has 27 truss pairs. On a rolling jig at grade, broken-back beams joined shippable trusses into stable pairs, kept them from spreading and provided convenient lifting points. Pairs were placed as self-supporting units spanning 120 ft (36.6 m).

11 At the ticketing front wall, two-pipe exterior columns have perforated battens like those on interior columns.

12 Folded-plate ridge skylights cast filtered light on roof soffits and brighten the ticketing hall below.

Typically, folded plate trusses are tied to prevent spreading, but at O'Hare the architects did not want visible ties to interfere with the clean ceiling planes. Thornton-Tomasetti designed a system of hidden members that prevent spreading while retaining Jahn's esthetic vision. Ten lines of steel beams, mitered and welded to follow the folded roof profile, keep each truss pair aligned and provide field-bolted splices to neighboring truss pairs (Fig.13). They also offered an unexpected construction opportunity by serving as lifting devices. By locating the "broken-back" beams above the trusses, they are concealed above the ribbed soffit panels and below the roofing system (Fig.14).

Martin Wolf was the Project Manager for Murphy / Jahn Architects. Wolf, now with Solomon, Cordwell and Buenz, Chicago, said the design demanded orchestrating and coordinating the structural systems in a fluid, articulated way. According to him, not many engineers would take the trouble to run calculations on so many variations. "The Thornton-Tomasetti philosophy is to get the best result for the buck."

13 Adjacent sets of folded plate truss assemblies were erected, then joined by the field-bolted valley splices between broken-back beams shown here during construction.

14 The completed folded-plate ticketing hall roof features long spans, skylights, daylit soffits and clean lines. Bottom chord crossties are avoided by using broken-back beams concealed above roof soffit panels.

For example, Wolf noted that the engineers proposed a purlin using a round pipe with a T-section welded along its length (Fig.16). In effect a variation on a wide-flange beam, it was more efficient than wide flanges or pipes alone, and allowed the use of smaller diameter, lighter pipes. It also provided a convenient place to make the glass roof connections that occur every 5 ft (1.5 m) along the framing system (Fig.18).

In the interest of esthetics, the architect rejected spray-on fireproofing for the X-bracing elements that form bands along the building envelope (Fig.17). Clean lines of exposed steel were maintained in a solution agreeable to Chicago code officials that included full sprinkler coverage of all the terminal buildings, a detailed fire engineering study, and specially designed columns for high load areas (Fig.15). Some exterior bracing uses 6 inch (152 mm) diameter rods with a special fireproofing finish.

The design team, which had worked together before, developed strategies for contractors and fabricators to make their concept work at the least cost. They collaborated on steel tolerances to make the fabricator's task easier while retaining the design integrity, and accepted alternative proposals for controlled welds that met esthetic requirements at a lower cost. The United Airlines Terminal, which opened in 1987, continues to be a landmark example of coordinated structural design and architecture.

15 Major building bracing is exposed and featured in the United Airlines O'Hare Terminal, as shown by this sculptured gusset plate at the intersection of four steel rod braces.

16 Shop-welding steel T-sections 3 1/2 inches (89 mm) deep atop 8 5/8 inch (219 mm) diameter steel pipes resulted in purlins that are more stable and less visually intrusive than wide-flange shapes, while also stronger and more practical for cladding connections than plain pipes.

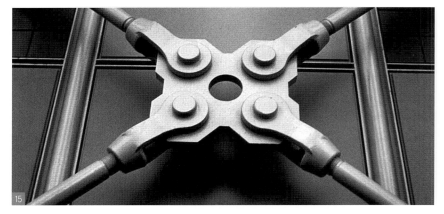

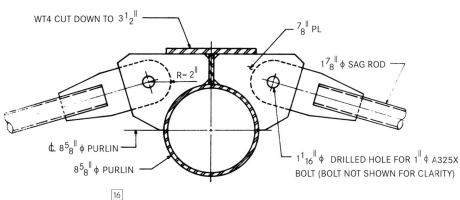

Owner
City of Chicago

Supervising Consultant
for O'Hare Development Program
O'Hare Associates

Design Architect
Murphy / Jahn Architects

Architect of Record
A. Epstein & Sons

Structural Engineers
**Thornton-Tomasetti Engineers &
A. Epstein & Sons**

General Contractor/Construction Manager
Turner Construction Co.

Other Team Members

Mechanical, Electrical & Plumbing Engineer
Syska & Hennessey
Steel Fabricator
Mosher Steel
Steel Erector
Broad, Vogt & Conant, Inc.

17 Exposed steel was permitted based on extensive use of fire suppression systems and a detailed fire protection study. The 40 ft (12.2 m) vault height in Concourse B is used here for a dinosaur display. A band of thin X-bracing crosses the concourse roof beyond the Brachiosaurus.

18 This detail view shows glazing mullions, sag rods, purlins, vault frames, hangers and concourse end roof framing working together in a consistent manner.

Overture Center for the Arts, Madison

The Overture Center for the Arts in Madison, Wisconsin, is a multi-use arts complex that fills an entire downtown city block. The project design effort solved a three-dimensional puzzle linking old and new performance spaces, including the new 2,300-seat Overture Hall (Fig.1). Cesar Pelli & Associates, New Haven, was the architect for the multi-faceted project. Fitting everything together was like assembling a Swiss watch, says Anne Haynes, project architect for Pelli. Multiple performance and lecture halls, galleries and museums were fitted within limited space around existing facilities, and linked to function together. However, from the outside that complexity is not evident.

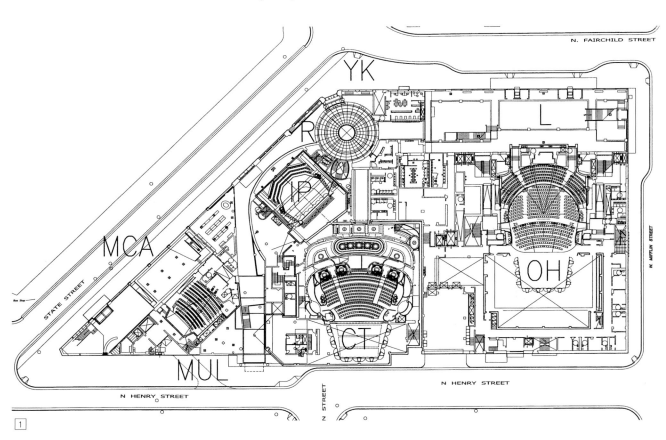

1 This plan of the Overture Center in Madison, Wisconsin, shows that the project brings together existing theaters, the corner façade of an old department store, new performance spaces and new circulation spaces. Construction is phased:

Overture Hall at right was completed in early 2004, while the entire project will be completed in 2006. The acute corner at lower left is glass-clad, and a larger glass façade wraps around the lobby of the Overture Hall at the top right corner. The historic Yost Kessenich façade is the new official entry to the Center.

CT Capitol Theater (existing, renovated).
IP Isthmus Playhouse (existing, renovated).
L Lobby of Overture Center.
MCA Madison Museum of Contemporary Art.
MUL Multi-use Lecture Hall.
OH Overture Hall.
R Rotunda.
YK Yost-Kessenich façade entry (existing, preserved).

The design intent was to relate to the street context, rather than to make a "global statement." Glass is used lavishly on the exterior, mixed with a Moorish-style tower and 100 ft (30.5 m) of façade from a former department store on the site (Figs.2-5). Both visual and performing art spaces tend to present a lot of blank outside walls, so Overture Center's mass is punctuated by "crystalline" glass elements.

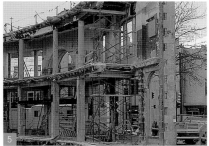

2 The stone cladding of this bank building was stripped and saved for future re-use before the building was demolished to make room for the Overture complex.

3 The Yost-Kessenich department store corner façade was preserved and re-used as the main entrance to Overture Center. It can be seen at lower right. Demolition is underway at left to make room for the new Overture Hall.

4,5 The Yost-Kessenich façade was temporarily braced by leaving one bay behind the street line.

Of the three main glass elements, the largest expanse forms the 80 ft (24.4 m) high, 100 ft (30.5 m) long lobby of Overture Hall (Fig.10). The panes are 9 ft (2.7 m) by 17 ft (5.2 m), and hang from the lobby roof. Thornton-Tomasetti Engineers had the task of keeping bracing to a minimum, while controlling deflections and carrying the glass weight. They made the structural elements invisible, says Haynes.

The site resembles a square with an extension that comes to a sharp "flatiron" angle, a shape typical of Madison where streets are not on a grid. At Overture Center, three stories of glass form both sides of the "flatiron" point. Visible through the glass is a dramatic staircase that leads to several levels of visual art spaces. The third glass element is the Center's domed rotunda entry sitting between Overture Hall's vast lobby and the glass "flatiron" edge (Figs.6-9).

The project was on a very fast track, and making the new and old portions mesh was a great esthetic challenge as well as a structural engineering and construction feat. Thornton-Tomasetti Engineers worked hard to make

6,7,8,9 Sunlight floods the rotunda by day. At night interior lighting makes the dome glow. Roof glazing over the rotunda was designed by MERO. The dome framing was assembled on a level surface and then lifted as a unit to top the glazed drum. The Capitol Theatre is at right and the Overture Hall is under construction at left.

10 The glass walls of the Overture Hall lobby façade are 80 ft (24.4 m) high and hang from the lobby roof framing.

every project participant happy. In such a situation, engineering technical competence is not enough. Instead, Haynes notes, "We feel a kinship with the engineers. They approach every project as a design problem, as do architects, and they help to shape space." Overture Hall is the complex's centerpiece. Acoustician Joseph Myers, of Kirkegaard Associates in Chicago, cites Thornton-Tomasetti's collaborative efforts: According to him, the issues were – again – not strictly structural; they required the engineer to be "willing to listen, to make things work." The most difficult challenge was to create a continuous 2 inch (51 mm) acoustic isolation space completely around the Hall while supporting overlapping elements (Figs.11,13,14,16). The acousticians mandated an 18 inch (457 mm) thick inside wall that was as high as 125 ft (38.1 m) (Fig.18). The engineers had to design a "box within a box" that could be constructed economically.

11 This cross-section of Overture Hall shows key acoustical engineering features.
A Lobby roof bears on pads on Overture Hall columns for acoustic isolation. See Figs.20,21.
B Attic space for proper Overture Hall acoustics.
C Stage House fly loft.
D Orchestra shell hinged side walls of plywood honeycomb on steel framing can retract into storage space at right.
E Pipe organ.
F Dressing rooms separated from stage by isolation joints.
G Orchestra lift pit.
H Plenum under seating provides air to the Hall
I Mechanical room outside of Hall.
J Acoustic isolation joints where Hall columns pass through non-Hall slabs
K Lobby bridges bear on isolation pads.
L Overture Hall lobby which is acoustically isolated from the hall.

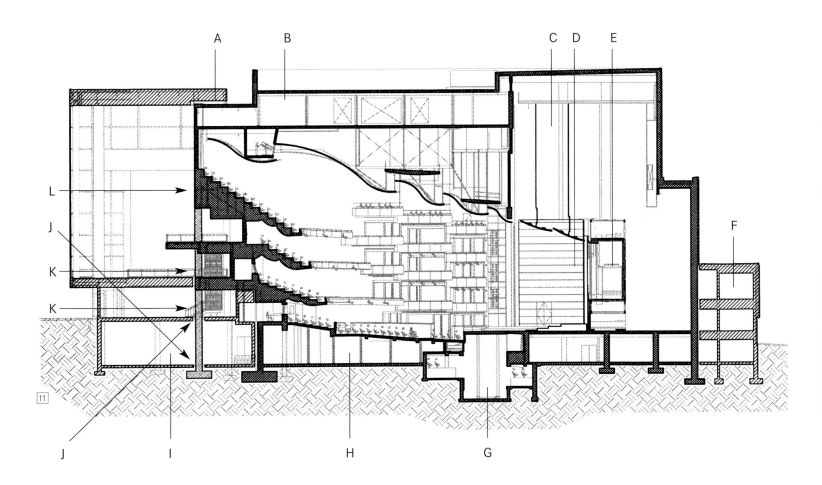

The outside wall incorporates structural load-bearing columns, and in some areas columns had to be threaded down to foundations without interfering with existing structures. The renovated Capitol Theater sits adjacent to the new hall, and no additional loads could be placed on or close to its foundations. The structural solution was to locate new foundations at an appropriate distance from the existing theater and to cantilever the Overture Hall floors (Fig.17).

12 The 125 ft (38.1 m) fly loft trusses at the top of the photo perform structural support and acoustic functions. Truss top chord will carry a concrete roof slab to block external sounds, and bottom chord will support a heavy ceiling to reflect low-frequency sound within the space. The trusses also carry rigging catwalks.

13,14 Steel angles were welded to plates embedded in concrete walls. Rubber pads on the steel shelf angles support the lobby floor slab while maintaining acoustic separation from Overture Hall.

15 For acoustic purposes, the engineers designed a "box within a box". Here the in-box columns rise through out-of-box slabs. View during construction from the lobby to the back of the balcony.

Three curved balconies were required within the performance hall. The highest balcony ends beyond the inside acoustic wall (Fig.19). To retain the necessary isolation, that balcony is supported by four columns that carry the loads down through the lobby floor and the mechanical room to separate footings while maintaining separation from those floors (Fig.15). For acoustic reasons, the mechanical ducts are larger than usual, and accommodating them in the structural framing was a design constraint for

16 The dramatically cantilevering roof of the Overture Hall lobby during construction. Its rear edge bears on Overture Hall through acoustic isolation joints. See Figs.20,21.

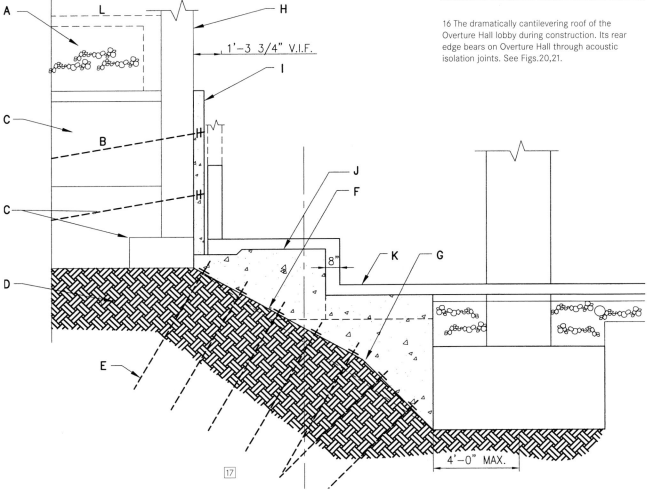

17 Great care was applied to construction of deeper footings adjacent to the existing Capitol Theater.

A Lightweight or expanded polystyrene foam block fill under new slab.

B Permanent tiebacks to restrain outward earth pressure under existing hall.

C Existing wall and column footings with unknown sizes and details.

D Undisturbed soil.

E Soil nails and soil anchors stabilize excavation slope.

F Line of maximum excavation was limited to not steeper than a 35 degree slope up from bottom of adjacent footings.

G Actual excavation line was kept to the minimum required to form the column footings.

H Existing basement wall.

I New wall reinforced as required for tieback system.

J Waterproofing.

K Relieved slab.

Thornton-Tomasetti. The solution, 125 ft (38.1 m) long trusses above the performance space, also enhances the acoustics; the concrete on the top and bottom chords and the air space within the trusses support low-frequency sounds and insulate the audience from noise generated by the mechanical ductwork (Fig.12). Ralph Jackson, Project Director with Potter Lawson and Flad, Executive Architects, also notes the "intricate" detailing. For example, some columns terminate as keeper stubs surrounded by horizontal and vertical elastomeric pads to transmit gravity and lateral loads across acoustic isolation joints where the lobby roof overlaps the performance space (Figs.20,21).

The Overture Hall geometry is very complex. For a typical building, structural engineers might design eight or ten standard concrete beams, but for this project, they had to design over 1,000 beams to address varying spans, different loads and strict depth limitations to clear mechanical systems and elaborate finishes.

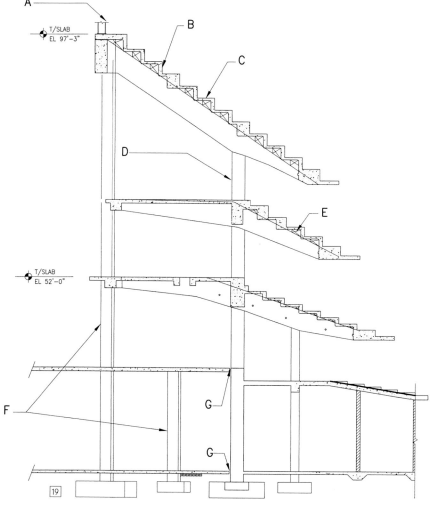

18 Most walls of the acoustic box surrounding Overture Hall are cast-in-place concrete, but behind the upper balcony masonry is used. A 12 inch (305 mm) thick masonry wall, grouted solid, provides the required mass and stiffness.

19 Overture Hall, balcony cross-section
A Steel column beyond.
B Round penetrations in slab for air distribution.
C Curved balcony seating slab.
D Concrete column.
E Formed penetration for air distribution.
F Concrete balcony support columns beyond.
G Acoustic isolation joints.

The entire Overture Center project called for reinforcing old columns and adding new beams and slabs to accommodate new building purposes. Two major transfers resulted from removing two columns to accommodate new circulation areas. It was a "surgical strike," says architect Haynes.

The $150 million complex was constructed in two phases. The Center includes Overture Hall, several theaters, galleries, a lecture hall, and two museums. Overture Hall was completed in early 2004, while the entire project is scheduled to be completed in 2006.

Owner
Overture Development Corporation

Design Architect
Cesar Pelli & Associates, Inc.

Executive Architect
Potter Lawson & Flad Architects LLC

Structural Engineer
Thornton-Tomasetti Engineers

General Contractor
J. H. Findorff & Son

Other Team Members

Mechanical, Electrical & Plumbing Engineer
Affiliated Engineers
Theater Consultant
Theatre Projects Consultants
Acoustical Consultant
Kirkegaard Associates

20 Lobby roof framing (shown bold) is acoustically isolated from, but laterally braced by, lower framing, in this detail with keeper pads on all four sides of the column.
B Full depth stiffeners to resist forces from guide brackets.
C Brackets surround column stub keeper to laterally restrain roof framing.

21 At perimeter columns, lobby roof framing (shown bold) is acoustically isolated but laterally braced by an offset stub.
A 12 inch (300 mm) deep wideflange steel cross-beams resist rolling effect of lateral restraint stub.
B 0.6 inch (15 mm) full depth stiffeners connect stub bracing tubes to cross-beams.
C Brackets surround keeper stub to laterally restrain roof framing.
D Full depth web stiffeners on both sides.
E W36 (900 mm deep) roof beam.
F 1.25 inch (32 mm) cap plate for gravity load through bearing pad.
G Acoustic isolation bearing pad 4 x 12 x 12 inches (100 x 300 x 300 mm) designed for 0.25 inch (6 mm) deflection under full service load (sustained load about 2/3 of full load).

Lucent Technologies Buildings, Chicago

Lucent Technologies makes a bold statement at its expanded research campus, two nearly identical buildings a half-mile apart in Naperville and Lisle, neighboring towns along the Illinois Research and Development Corridor west of Chicago. Both buildings have matching office wings extending from opposite sides of a central lobby and matching skylights (Figs.1,2). Within this unifying theme, each building is given its own identity by highly original, and radically different, architectural and structural designs for the two lobby atria.

The architect was Kevin Roche John Dinkeloo Associates of Hamden, Connecticut. Thornton-Tomasetti Engineers was the structural engineer. Both buildings feature designs that demanded a high level of creative collaboration between architect and structural engineer. Philip Kinsella, the architect's Managing Principal, says the engineers were "sympathetic to the design goals, creative and flexible." At times, their "suggested solutions and alternative approaches resulted in a more refined expression of those goals." The collaboration yielded solutions that retained design intent while respecting constructibility and durability requirements.

1 This aerial view of the Lucent Lisle site shows two wings angled about a central glass atrium, with parking decks beyond the wings. Both Lisle and Naperville have similar wing arrangements.

The project was complex in many ways. To get competitive prices, the buildings were bid separately. As a result, each building had its own steel fabricator; one fabricator produced shop drawings by hand drafting, while the other used state-of-the-art 3-D computer programs. Both exposed steel entryways have extremely intricate geometry and connection details with unforgiving tolerances, requiring the precise integration of steel fabrication and erection procedures. Steel tolerances were less than an inch overall, accumulated over four or more joints, because the connections between members were welded rather than bolted.

The lobbies are emphatically the focal points of the buildings. For the Lisle building the architects created an elliptical, 120 ft (36.6 m) wide, glass-clad, steel pipe drum. The drum is sliced at a 45 degree angle and roofed with a concave surface, evoking a satellite dish (Fig.3). At its highest point, the roof soars 115 ft (35.1 m), well above the five-story wings on each side (Fig.4). An entrance canopy, framed between the drum and a freestanding pipe column that stands sentinel at the front tip of the building, handles roof drainage (Figs.5,6).

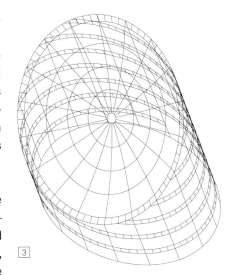

3

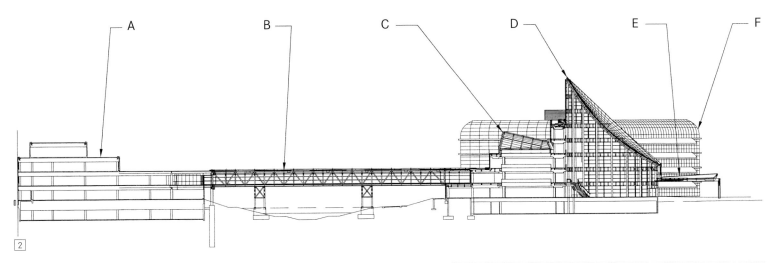

2

2 A section along the Lisle building line of symmetry shows key points.
A Existing building.
B New pedestrian bridge.
C Skylight (common to both locations).
D Glazed drum atrium.
E Entry canopy.
F Building wing beyond (common to both locations).

3 A round "dish" roof, set at a 45 degree slope, defines the elliptical drum of the Lisle entry atrium.

4 Both sites have skylights like the one in the foreground, but the Lisle drum stands 115 ft (35.1 m) tall, well above adjacent office wings.

To achieve the design, Thornton-Tomasetti conceived of exposed steel pipes creating a virtual membrane for the roof, supported by a hierarchy of visually logical structural shapes (Fig.7). The engineers designed tilted roof members with sufficient flexural stiffness to counteract the effects of self-weight acting at the 45 degree angle, in addition to unbalanced wind and snow loads (Fig.8). The roof's radial ribs were shop-fabricated in "pie slice"

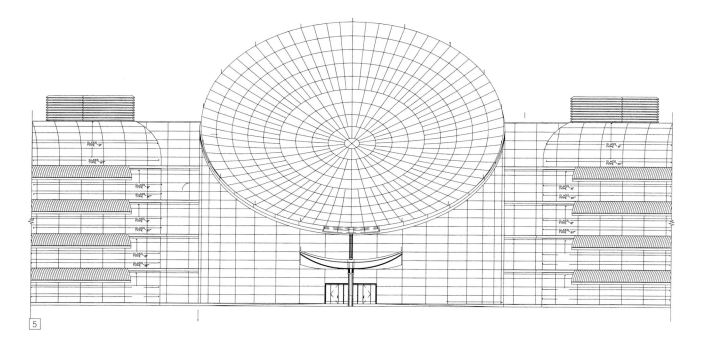

5 The sculptural entry canopy is positioned to receive Lisle atrium roof drainage.

6 Lisle entry plan
A Glazed atrium drum.
C 16 inch (406 mm) diameter steel atrium column.
D Entry canopy outline.
E Steel grating over drainage reception pit.
F Metal deck roofing support.
G Free-form steel plate girder.
H Trapezoidal steel box girder.
I 24 inch (610 mm) diameter pipe column.
S Tilted barrel vault skylight.
W Building wing roof.

7 A hierarchy of pipe diameters, from large columns to small infill beams, establishes the visual rhythm of the Lisle entry atrium.

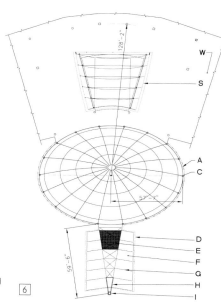

126

segments, and assembled and welded on site to a central hub (Figs.9,10). Seven curved, 42 inch (1,067 mm) deep rings of Vierendeel trusses along the drum's perimeter resist its lateral loads (Figs.11,14). Maintaining precise geometry among all pieces during erection was critical, both for column verticality and for proper fit-up (Figs.12,13).

8 Cross section of half the Lisle atrium roof "dish" showing the hierarchy of steel pipes used to hold desired shape when tilted.
A 16 inch (406 mm) diameter
  steel atrium perimeter ring pipe.
B 8.6 inch (219 mm) diameter by 0.9 inch
  (22 mm) thick Vierendeel chord and vertical
  pipes.
C 16 inch (406 mm) diameter pipe columns.
D 8 inch (203 mm) diameter
  roof "dish" radial pipe.

E 12 inch (305 mm) diameter edge pipe, linked
  to perimeter ring to form Vierendeel truss band.
F 6 inch (152 mm) diameter circumferential
  infill ring pipe.
G Steel WT glazing support varies from WT 9
  (229 mm deep) atop rings (F) to WT 4
  (102 mm deep) atop (A).
H Hub at center is a stiffened box built up from
  steel plates. See Fig.10.
J Joint in drum columns with guide lugs for field
  alignment prior to welding. See Fig.13.

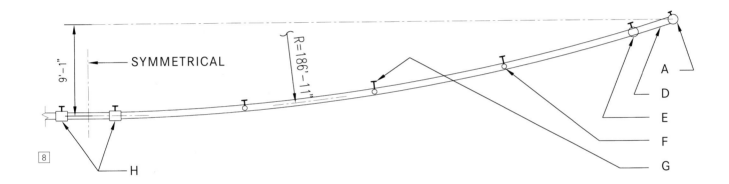

9 The Lisle atrium central hub was set on temporary shoring, and pre-assembled "pie slice" sectors of the roof "dish" were then placed and welded to the hub stubs visible in the foreground. The welded joints had limited fit-up tolerance, requiring very accurate steel detailing and fabrication.

10 At the central hub plan detail, all radial pipes are spliced like the one weld shown. See Fig.8 legend.

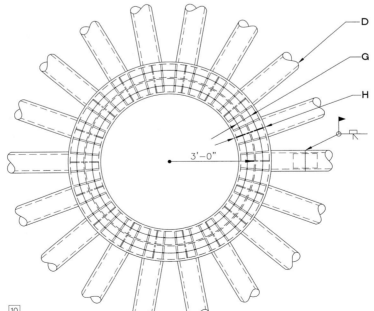

The central lobby at Naperville is lower than at Lisle, but equally dramatic and even more structurally demanding. The entrance is a vaulted glass canopy between the flanking wings. Structurally, the lobby is a truncated barrel vault 126 ft (38.4 m) long, supported by four cantilevered structural steel tri-cord trusses (Fig.15). The canopy cantilevers 45 ft (13.7 m), with the truss back ends

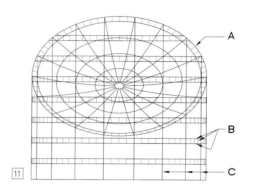

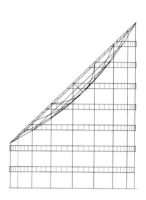

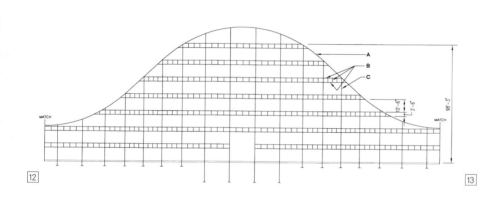

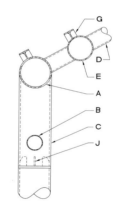

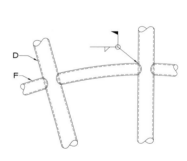

11 Lateral stability of the Lisle atrium is provided by seven Vierendeel truss bands encircling the vertical glazed walls. See Fig.8 for legend.

12 A tilted roof plane intersecting an elliptical drum results in complex geometry that posed a steel detailing challenge, as seen in this "unfolded" view of the Lisle atrium drum framing.

13 Pipe sizes were selected to minimize interference at joints. Alignment lugs were provided where possible to speed erection. See Fig.8 legend.

14 Vierendeel drum bands and graduated pipe sizes provide an open structural system with an organized, unified appearance for the Lisle atrium.

attaching to the building (Fig.19). It is laterally supported by a trussed portal frame (Fig.17) and a cross-braced spine (Fig.18). While the two inner trusses align with the roof surface generator lines, the outer trusses run at an angle to the roof (Fig.20). As a result, those trusses twist along their axes to follow the curved roof surface, and their pipe members curve about two axes (Fig.16).

15 Four tri-chord steel trusses run from the main building to a portal frame, and then cantilever 45 ft (13.7 m) beyond. The glazed roof mullions follow the generator lines for the roof surface, but the lower trusses cross those lines on a skew.

Purlins were hand-fit to the two top chords of each truss, evenly spaced and pitched so that glass would fit properly (Fig.21). In the entire canopy design, no two pieces of steel are alike; the architect, engineers and steel fabricator shared 3-D computer models to perform the design and construction. Fast-track construction at Naperville made close coordination of this structure especially critical.

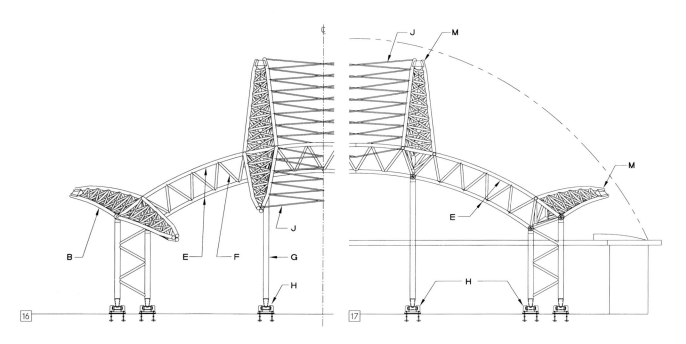

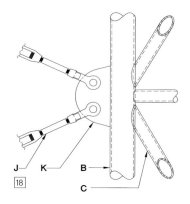

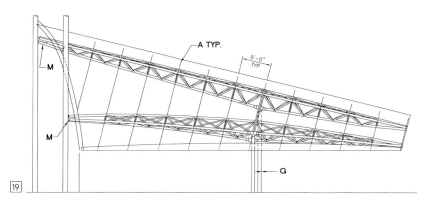

16 The lower truss is twisted in this view along the Naperville roof axis. See Fig.19 legend.

17 The Naperville entry atrium is stabilized perpendicular to its axis by a trussed portal frame, linked to the full roof length by an X-braced "spine."

18 Clevises and mid-length turnbuckles (shown closer to ends here) permit proper tensioning of the stainless steel bracing rods forming the roof spine.

19 Supporting a sloping, truncated slice of a round cylinder, the Naperville glazed roof is supported on curved HSS rectangular steel tubes perpendicular to the cylinder axis.

Legend for all Lucent Naperville drawings:
A Rectangular steel tube purlins HSS 8 inches (203 mm) wide by 16 inches (406 mm) tall.
B 8 inch (203 mm) diameter steel pipe chord of main truss.
C 5 inch (127 mm) diameter pipe diagonals of main truss.
D Enlarged chord "can" for connection forces at main truss intersections.

E Transverse portal truss 8 inch (203 mm) diameter steel pipe chords.
F 5 inch (127 mm) diameter pipe diagonals of portal truss.
G 12 inch (305 mm) diameter pipe column legs.
H Pivot base at legs allows canopy to "grow" and "shrink" towards and away from building with temperature changes.
J 0.7 inch (18 mm) diameter stainless steel rod X-bracing along canopy "spine."
K 1.25 inch (32 mm) thick gusset plate receives bracing clevis fitting.
M Connections to main building columns provide roof stability along its axis.

Both research centers have a central, sloping barrel vault skylight reminiscent of the Naperville canopy (Figs.22,23). They further emphasize natural light and visual openness with continuous glass bands that wrap around the office wings. Inside, 10 ft (3.1 m) wide exterior corridors are cantilevered from columns set 11 ft (3.4 m) back from the façade. The walkway ceilings and supporting members taper upward toward the exterior glass walls, maximizing views and light penetration.

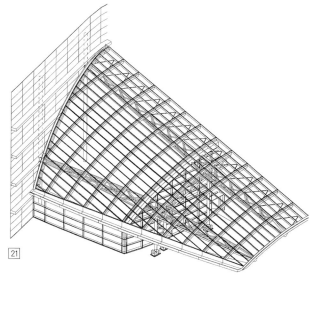

21

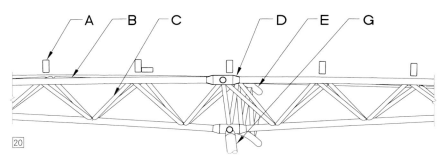

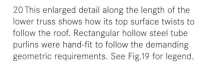

20

20 This enlarged detail along the length of the lower truss shows how its top surface twists to follow the roof. Rectangular hollow steel tube purlins were hand-fit to follow the demanding geometric requirements. See Fig.19 for legend.

21 In this half-width view, the upper tri-chord truss follows roof mullions defining a single plane. The lower truss crosses mullions and must twist to fit under the roof. The portal frame leg pivots are also visible.

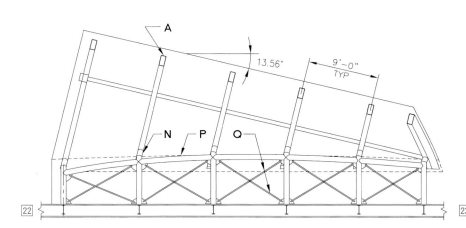

22

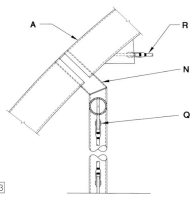

23

22 The central skylight in both the Lisle and Naperville buildings is a tilted, truncated cylindrical section that echoes the Naperville entry roof in a subtle design link.
Legend for both skylight drawings
A Rectangular steel tube purlins HSS 8 inches (203 mm) wide by 16 inches tall (406 mm).
N 8 inch (203 mm) diameter dog-leg (mitered) connection pipe to purlins.

P 8 inch (203 mm) diameter steel pipe girt for wall framing.
Q 1 inch (25.4 mm) diameter steel rod X-bracing with clevis to gusset plate.
R 0.7 inch (18 mm) diameter stainless steel bracing for lateral stability.

23 Skylight wall-to-roof framing separated bracing planes and used mitered posts to handle potentially complex intersections as simply as possible.

The design strives to enhance the exchange of ideas among scientists, engineers and managers by offering circulation and communication spaces along the airy corridors. The building's eccentrically-braced lateral load-resisting system is located at the elevator cores at the ends of the wings, further enhancing openness and light, and satisfying the design mandate for large column-free bays. The offices are inboard of the perimeter corridors. The wing exteriors have curved stainless steel and reflective glass sun-shades that stretch horizontally across the façade, adding visual interest but necessitating complicated connection details (Fig.25).

At the top of each wing, the 5th floor glass roof curves back from the façade. Lucent, the New Jersey-based telecommunications giant, opened their Illinois research and development buildings in 2000 (Fig.24).

Owner
Lucent Technologies

Architect
Kevin Roche John Dinkeloo Associates

Structural Engineer
Thornton-Tomasetti Engineers

General Contractor
Ragnar Benson

Other Team Members

Mechanical, Electrical & Plumbing Engineer
Cosentini Associates
Steel Fabricators
Lisle Wings
Merrill Iron and Steel Inc.
Lisle Lobby
Chicago Ornamental Iron Co.
Naperville Wings
Zalk Joseph Fabricators LLC
Naperville Lobby
MTH Industries

24 At night the perimeter corridors at the Lucent facilities in Lisle (pictured) and Naperville provide an inviting glow.

25 Long building elevations housing labs and offices are enlivened by curved stainless steel sun shades.

World Financial Center Winter Garden, New York

New York City's World Financial Center Winter Garden, originally designed in 1981, is a gem in glass and steel. A public space nestled between two office towers in the five-building, $1.5 billion World Financial Center (WFC), it visually links the former World Trade Center site on the east with the Hudson River on the west (Fig.1). Architect Cesar Pelli won the design competition for the WFC project with a composition that brilliantly transitions

1 The Winter Garden was oriented to work with the World Trade Center beyond as part of a larger composition, the World Financial Center.

from the Hudson River shoreline to the World Trade Center's bluff towers (Fig.2). His design evokes a busy cityscape with just four office towers by using four different façade types with different proportions of stone and glass, and by changing types at multiple setbacks (Figs.3,4). The Winter Garden was repaired and reconfigured for new traffic patterns after the September 11, 2001 attacks on the World Trade Center.

The original Winter Garden design functioned both as the centerpiece for the 14 acre (5.7 hectare) World Financial Center project and as the main pedestrian entry point by a bridge over West Street (Figs.5,6). An immense glass-covered public gathering place with shops and restaurants, the roof

2 Cesar Pelli's design massed World Financial Center towers to transition from the bluff World Trade Center to the Hudson shoreline.

3 Setbacks and low-rise extensions break up the façades of the office towers, as seen here under construction.

4 Sunset glinting off the World Financial Center towers highlights the different mixes in glazing and stone cladding used to evoke a century of different building types.

over the 45,000 square foot (4,181 square meter) atrium has four arched vaults with 2,000 panes of glass held in place by a latticework of steel trusses (Fig.7). Inside, a monumental staircase at the east end flows to a marble floor shaded by ranks of stately palm trees and what may be the world's largest glass wall, 106 ft (32.3 m) wide and 119 ft (36.3 m) tall (Fig.8). Just beyond the window-wall, a public promenade runs along the Hudson River.

The engineering challenge was to create large open spans with minimal visual weight. Thornton-Tomasetti Engineers developed structural systems that met Pelli's esthetic requirements in an economical and unobtrusive manner. Four telescoping barrel vaults are supported on 16 trussed arches that spring from bearings at the fourth floor, 57 ft (17.4 m) above the main

5 A broad covered pedestrian bridge led from the World Trade Center to the Winter Garden as gateway to the World Financial Center development.

6 Two pedestrian bridges crossed West Street. Twilight highlights the different façades used on the office towers.

7 Too large to capture in a conventional photo, the Winter Garden half-dome end, four barrel vaulted roof segments, and iconic palm trees appear in this distorted "fish eye" view.

floor. The highest vault, standing 128 ft (39 m) above the floor, is flanked by two 118 ft (36 m) high vaults, one of which meets the folded plate window-wall to the west. A 108 ft (32.9 m) high vault at the street side meets a 55 ft (16.8 m) diameter half-dome at the entrance.

8 Semi-circular trussed arches span over the sweeping, palm-shaded Winter Garden floor and its end wall with Hudson River views.

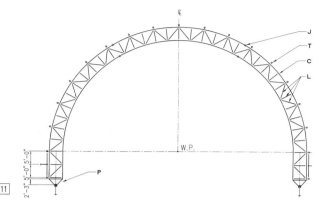

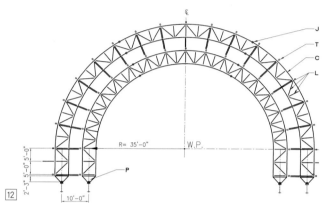

Each vault consists of parallel arched trusses carrying perpendicular tubular steel RHS 5 x 7 x 3/16 inch purlins (127 x 178 x 5 mm) for glazing support (Fig.11). Double trussed arches occur at vault steps (Fig.12). All steel trusses were assembled by shop-welding into large erection units and then field-spliced for a clean appearance. With steel WT 8 and WT 7 (203 mm and 178 mm deep) chords and double angle diagonals with legs 3 1/2 inches (89 mm) and smaller, the arches are delicate in appearance as they span up to 110 ft (33.5 m) between bearings.

The half-dome uses an unusual configuration to minimize visual clutter and resolve forces. Instead of dome ribs radiating in plan from a hub at the vault crown, the arrangement is turned 90 degrees: quarter-circle trusses radiate from the low roof level (Fig.9). This way they meet the end vault truss like inter-truss ties, and their visually dense point of convergence is low and less visible. In addition, because they act as beams and not thrust-bearing ribs, the quarter-circle trusses frame to a semi-circular bridging

9 In this original construction photograph, half-dome trusses radiate from a floor-level work point, rather than the dome peak, to keep the roof as transparent as possible.

10 Radial quarter-circle trusses rise from a central hub and meet the lower arch geometric pattern in this computer model rendering of the roof end half-dome.

11 Roof vault arches vary in radius but follow a common design.
C Chords, steel WT 8 or WT 7 (203 mm and 178 mm deep) sections, depending on location.
J Field joint locations between shop-fabricated sections.
L Double angle diagonals and radials, with 3 1/2 inch (89 mm) legs and smaller.
P Pin bearing detail at Level 4.
T Steel tube purlins, RHS 5 x 7 x 3/16 inches (127 x 178 x 5 mm).

12 At vault steps, one arch carries the high vault and the other, the low vault. The trusses are linked to limit differential deflection, but work independently for strength. For legend, see above.

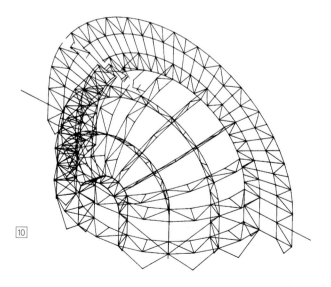

line rather than a conventional heavy steel-plate hub (Fig.10). In contrast, an adjacent World Financial Center tower has a true dome (Fig.13). It was built of radial trusses (Figs.14,15), erected as "pie slices" with steel plate outer shell and angles for blocking to sheathing (Fig.16). During construction each "slice" temporarily spanned to a shored central hub. The shore was later removed (Fig.17). The difference in visual congestion between the tower dome and the vault half-dome framing is clear.

The engineers were asked to resist roof arch thrusts without tie rods or abutments that would have compromised the architect's light and airy design concept. They also could not rely on adjacent towers, as tower sway would deform the arches. The solution was to use the fourth level mechanical room floor framing, a U in plan. Steel diagonals were provided beneath its concrete floor to create a stiff horizontal curved truss that resists vault arch thrusts, just as a horseshoe resists attempts to straighten it out. To avoid sway-induced deformations, an expansion joint separates that floor

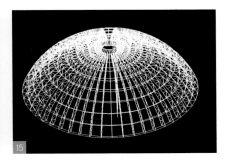

13 The domed rooftop mechanical room, atop an adjacent World Financial Center office tower, provides a clear contrast to the half-dome framing system of the Winter Garden below it.

14 Radial trussed ribs frame the office tower rooftop dome to provide column-free space for large pieces of mechanical equipment.

16 The office dome was erected in prefabricated "pie slices," each with several trussed ribs, curved steel plate deck, and cleats for later mounting of nailers, and wood decking for copper sheathing. "Slices" temporarily span from edge to a shored central hub.

15 For reasonable spans of the steel plate deck, tower dome trussed ribs are closely spaced as shown in this computer model rendering.

17 Sized to allow all ribs to meet it, the office dome hub shows visual congestion where dome ribs converge.

18 Level 4, a mechanical room floor, is trussed to create a rigid "horseshoe" in plan that resists the outward thrust of roof arches without visually objectionable tie rods crossing the Winter Garden space. The clear span shown is pin-to-pin of roof arches.
EJ Expansion joint between Winter Garden and the adjacent office tower.
H Horizontal thrust direction from roof arches under gravity load.
R Reinforcing diagonal member to create the floor truss.
T Adjacent office tower on each side.
WG Winter Garden space.

from one adjacent tower (Fig.18). The other tower provides lateral stability without resisting lateral arch thrust. The horizontal U-truss inner edges sit on eight twin-leg composite steel-and-concrete columns that bear on caissons to bedrock (Fig.19). Each leg of the horseshoe is 175 ft (53.4 m) long, and the clear space between legs varies from 70 to 110 ft (21.3 to 33.5 m) to match the arch spans.

For the huge glass end wall it was important to minimize member sizes for transparency, while allowing free in-plane movement relative to the walls and roof that provide lateral support. An early proposal had horizontal trusses behind the wall (Fig.20). In the final design, the engineers used its articulated surface to advantage: by incorporating a vertical horseshoe truss in the sloping surface that links two vertical planes 8.5 ft (2.6 m) apart, no projecting trusses were needed (Fig.21).

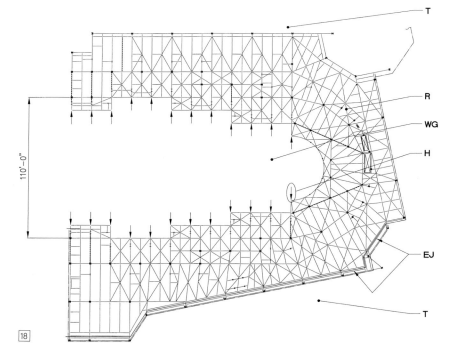

19 Arches landing on the edges of the Winter Garden space are carried by deep steel girders spanning to twinned concrete-encased steel columns, as seen during original construction.

Shaped gusset plates knife into double-channel truss diagonals to make nearly invisible connections (Fig.22). The truss receives wind loads from horizontal W18 (450 mm deep) mullions and spans 70 ft (21.3 m) from grade to the roof arch work point elevation. At the work point elevation, a horizontal truss formed by a W18 (450 mm deep) tie and a broken-back mullion spans wind loads to lateral braces 96 ft (29.3 m) apart. Intricate isolation joint details stabilize the roof out-of-plane while allowing free movement in-plane.

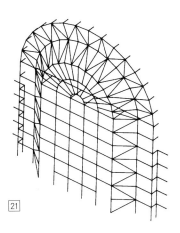

The site also presented subterranean difficulties. The Winter Garden is located partially on soil fill and partially over a commuter rail line tunnel. To minimize pressure on the tunnel, steel trusses span over it and bear on caissons on either side. Elsewhere, column loads bear on caissons extending 60 ft (18.3 m) down to rock.

20 An early study model shows trusses projecting into the Winter Garden from the west glazed wall. The projection was eliminated by clever use of the wall shape itself.

21 The final end wall design uses offset planes to advantage: a flat truss is able to span wind loads to upper and lower supports.

22 Careful detailing provided end wall framing with virtually invisible connections.

23 The main connecting bridge over West Street originally led pedestrians to the east end of the Winter Garden.

In 2001, World Trade Center debris broke every glass pane in the Winter Garden roof, and falling steel penetrated three of the vaults (Fig.24). Structurally, the worst damage was at the northeast curve of the horizontal horseshoe arch. Debris from the attack sat in a pile 55 ft (16.8 m) deep, fortuitously supporting the destroyed portion of this arch and temporarily forestalling collapse. Architect Pelli and Thornton-Tomasetti Engineers were among those called back to assess the damage and work on the reconstruction. The engineers immediately designed a shoring and bracing system to fend off collapse, and the contractors began removing debris, restoring damaged welded steel members, and replacing glass. The pedestrian bridge that once joined the Winter Garden to the World Trade Center was also gone (Figs.23,25). In all, 100% of the laminated glazing and 20% of the steel structural members in the vaulted expanse had to be replaced, along with several columns. Clever construction methods, including an overhead crane system, sped the work. Pelli designed a striking new glass façade, 112 ft (34.1 m) wide and 59 ft (18 m) high, creating a ground-level entrance to the building (Fig.28). The reconstruction cost $50 million, compared to the $65 million cost of the original Winter Garden.

24 The Winter Garden was extensively damaged on September 11, 2001, but stood and was practical to repair. This photo shows an early stage in the process.

25 Destruction of pedestrian bridges in the September 11, 2001 attacks required reconfiguration of the adjacent Winter Garden façade and floors to create a ground-level entry. This repair photo also shows the overhead crane system used by the contractors to re-glaze the roof several times faster than for the original construction.

Rafael Pelli, of Cesar Pelli & Associates, led the reconstruction process. He praised Thornton-Tomasetti Engineers for its "enormous ingenuity and precision" at the chaotic site. In view of the complicated issues of stabilization and the furious pace of the schedule, "they showed imagination and a willingness to explore alternative structural solutions under extreme duress. The number one priority was the recovery work at Ground Zero across the way, and we relied on them for their willingness to reconsider anything and everything, and their ability to see the big picture, and still think about costs and the schedule."

The Winter Garden first opened in 1988. Extensively damaged in the September 11, 2001 attack on the Twin Towers, it was rebuilt and reopened exactly one year later. With its subsequent restoration and adaptation to new pedestrian traffic patterns, the Winter Garden remains a focal point, both visually and functionally, for the Hudson shoreline in lower Manhattan (Figs.26,27).

WORLD FINANCIAL CENTER

Owner/Developer
Olympia & York

Architect
Cesar Pelli & Associates, Inc.

Structural Engineer
Thornton-Tomasetti Engineers

Mechanical, Electrical & Plumbing
Flack + Kurtz

WINTER GARDEN RECONSTRUCTION

Owner
Brookfield Properties Corp.

Design Architect
Cesar Pelli & Associates, Inc.

Production Architect
Adamson Associates

Structural Engineer
Thornton-Tomasetti Engineers

Construction Contractor
Turner Construction Co.

Scaffolding and Shoring
Atlantic-Heydt Corp.

Mechanical, Electrical & Plumbing Engineer
Flack + Kurtz

26,27 Although the view behind it has changed, revealing the Woolworth Building, the Winter Garden has maintained its role as a focal point for circulation and pedestrian activities on the Hudson shoreline in lower Manhattan.

28 A new street-level entry to the Winter Garden is signaled by this taut glass skin, a clear contrast with the existing stone-clad building panels surrounding it.

Long-Span Structures

Arenas have been part of the urban landscape since ancient Rome, proof of the enduring interest in public entertainment. A recent wave of arena construction has occurred in the U.S. for several reasons. Beyond providing improved facilities for spectator sports and entertainment presentations, arenas are also business enterprises, and extensive modern luxury suites form an essential part of the financial package. They are also often intended as drivers for urban renewal and economic development. Today's arenas are very high-tech and, unlike their predecessors, modern arenas generally have long-span roofs for column-free viewing. All of these factors affect their architecture and the engineering design that supports them.

Realizing the architectural concept is always the principal project challenge for structural engineers, followed closely by the design of the long-span roof itself. Supporting great spans at the lowest possible cost is the overriding goal of most arena structural designs. The roof must carry heavy loads, including snow loads, scoreboards, and the massive sound and lighting systems of modern concert extravaganzas. The requisite luxury suites also affect the structural design. And owners want the best possible sightlines with minimal obstruction from structural columns. They also want their projects completed on a fast track basis, the sooner to begin generating income.

Arena design has become a specialty niche for Thornton-Tomasetti Engineers. Over the years, the firm's engineers developed a highly efficient tension-tied truss to support arena roofs. They use much shallower trusses than in traditional designs, and, consequently, the structural system weighs less. All its members work at or near maximum stress, as opposed to the "brute force" of traditional 30 ft (9.1 m) to 40 ft (12.2 m) deep trusses. This means they must be precisely designed and analyzed for all possible load combinations including drifts, uplift and rigging point loads.

This system works well when three key conditions are met: the roof shape follows structurally appropriate geometry, the bending moments from applied loads are reasonably consistent with the roof shape, and the tension-tie level can be integrated with lighting and rigging systems. Structurally appropriate geometry includes barrel vaults, domes, or combinations of those shapes. Consistent bending moments occur when the moment diagram is largest where the structure can be deepest, as at mid-span of a barrel-vaulted roof, and when unbalanced loads are a small fraction of total loads. The firm's engineers have customized variations of the tied-arch truss to meet special requirements for different arenas. They also design with practical construction in mind, especially the roof erection sequence. Maximizing repetition and minimizing falsework that could impede other site work aids on-time completion. Economy of construction is further enhanced by designs that permit roof construction to begin before completion of structural framing below.

This section of the book includes five arenas with roof designs that taxed the limits of structural creativity. The stadium Soldier Field in Chicago that accompanies them may seem simpler since it has no roof. However, the structure is a retrofit with a highly unconventional design, including rear-leaning cantilevers that were as challenging as a roof structure.

At the Pepsi Center in Denver, the roof presented an elongated oval, and a swift and economical structural solution had to be found for the fast-track project. At the Gaylord Arena in Nashville and the Philips Arena in Atlanta, the architectural concepts included unusual roof shapes that posed structural design complexities far beyond the typical. At Ford Field in Detroit, the gargantuan size was one major challenge.

The Pepsi Center in Denver had a typically short time frame for design and construction. The owner set a strict 21-month schedule with a fixed budget. The engineers worked closely with architects HOK Sport+Venue+Event to establish a roof profile well suited to highly efficient tied arches, a "racetrack" with two end half-domes joined to a central barrel vault. Radial ribs support the half-domes by spanning from perimeter to a central spine. The spine is carried by tied arches that share tension ties through an inverted pyramidal king post. The resulting design is highly efficient, a roof that uses only 17 psf (87 kg / square meter) of steel.

The Gaylord Arena, is a multi-use space, designed by HOK Sport+Venue+Event to highlight country music motifs emblematic of that city. While the barrel vaulted roof profile seemed well-suited to a straightforward tied arch structure, the desire for multiple, stepped and sloped roof segments did not. A further complication was a seating bowl that cantilevers beyond the lower building footprint. The architect's concept required a mixture of structural approaches to provide a constructible frame that follows the complicated geometry. Trussed rigid frames bend up from below the seats to help carry the roof, reducing the distance that mid-span drop-in trusses must cover. This reduces the mid-span truss depth to a shippable size. The engineers conducted eight analyses to determine roof behavior during construction to better guide the contractor.

In Atlanta, the Philips Arena has a striking layered roof. The architects, Arquitectonica and HOK Sport, intended the odd angles and slopes of the roof layers to make a bold visual statement to viewers who look down from the tall buildings that surround the arena. This roof configuration was also not well suited to optimized tied-arch long spans, but it offered other opportunities for structural efficiency. The steps between roof levels accommodate deep trusses that frame out the central arena roof, and the engineers took advantage of a unique asymmetrical seating bowl design to reduce the typical spans of infill trusses by providing twin tension-tied arches sitting on one side of the arena. In this way most roof framing uses shallower trusses of shippable depth.

At Ford Field, size was the principal issue. With football seating bowl dimensions nearly double those of typical basketball or hockey arenas, this arena in Detroit, is one of the largest covered sports facilities in the United States. The owner ruled out any columns within the viewing area. The SmithGroup architects worked with the structural engineers to devise a system of unusually large trusses that addressed fabrication, erection and stability issues. For lateral stability they engage so-called supercolumns that avoid historic buildings below.

Soldier Field is an imaginative retrofit of a stadium built to commemorate soldiers who died in World War I, and anchors a larger urban waterfront improvement. Current sports economics drove the owners to expand seating capacity. The old concrete structure with its classic colonnades was a landmark and therefore sacrosanct. None of the new structure could add loads to the old stadium, so the engineering was a delicate proposition. Due to the narrow space between colonnades, providing a modern facility seemed impossible, but Boston architects Wood + Zapata, with the Chicago firm of Lohan Caprile Goettsch, conceived a unique design: a broad low funnel set on a donut hole, the playing field. The addition has ample room for seating and skyboxes. To avoid contact with the old colonnades, the seating supports reach far beyond and above them. To execute this bold concept, engineers designed several extreme cantilevers with very shallow steel members. The hybrid structure is an exemplar of ideal urban architecture that combines old and new with grace and integrity.

All the structures in this section illustrate engineering challenges and innovative and cost-effective solutions. They also demonstrate how the structural system selected impacts constructibility, facilitating expedited construction schedules through thoughtful design.

Gaylord Arena, Nashville

The Gaylord Entertainment Center in Nashville, Tennessee, combines structural complexity with vivid musical motifs. The architect, George Heinlein, conceived a unique building whose shape mimics an open music box, a steel lattice tower symbolizing radio broadcasts, and a horn-shaped rehearsal hall that "heralds the renaissance of Nashville" (Fig.1).

Urban renewal was a goal of Nashville officials who held the 1993 design competition for the complex. The winning entry was by architect Hellmuth, Obata + Kassabaum, Kansas City, Missouri. Heinlein was the team leader and is now in private practice with Heinlein Schrock Stearns, Kansas City.

1 The unique shapes of Gaylord Entertainment Center evoke a music box lid starting to open, a latticework radio broadcasting tower and a horn (beyond) in keeping with a facility intended as a musical performance venue.

Gaylord's curved and tilted three-level roof posed a design quandary for the structural engineers because of its complex geometry. There are three levels of seats at the highest level; the middle level has two tiers of seats, and the lowest level has one. The highest roof level rises 130 ft (39.6 m) above ground level; at the lowest end, the roof is 100 ft (30.5 m) high. Architect Heinlein says, "The Gaylord Arena had the most complex geometry of any project we ever worked on, and we couldn't have done it without the collaboration of Thornton-Tomasetti Engineers. We both tapped our creativity to the utmost."

The design team developed a daring solution in which several structural systems interact to make the unusual architectural geometry work. Around the arena perimeter, they used "boomerang" trusses, cantilever trusses, triangulated pipe trusses, and two 6 ft (1.8 m) diameter columns that sit at either end of the performance stage at the lowest end.

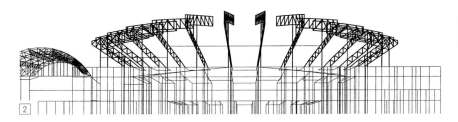

2,3 These "boomerang" trusses each stand on two legs for erection stability, while forming the highest level seating bowl and starting the roof structure.

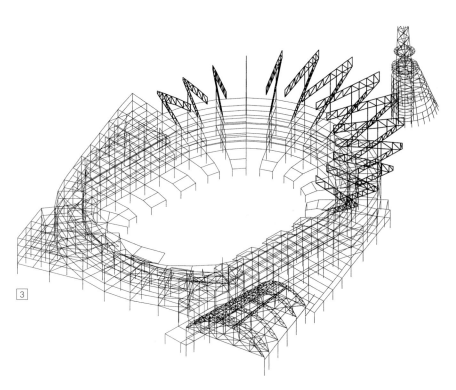

147

4 Horseshoe trusses between "boomerangs" stabilized them for application of roofing loads.

5 Horseshoe trusses are in place, and mid-section cantilevered trusses are being erected.

6 Precast seating units were placed on the lower legs of "boomerang" trusses soon after they were erected to speed the overall arena construction schedule.

At the high roof section, 14 "boomerang" trusses stand like giant number sevens (Figs.2,3). Since these are self-supporting elements, the contractor could install the top seating tier of precast, prestressed units early in the process (Fig.6). A triangular space truss of pipes ties the boomerang tops together in a horseshoe plan and redistributes forces (Figs.4,5). The pipe truss also forms the faceted elliptical edge of the high roof – the "open music box lid." The horseshoe/boomerang system also allowed early installation of a mechanical room; its dead load counters loads from the roof at the top of the "boomerangs."

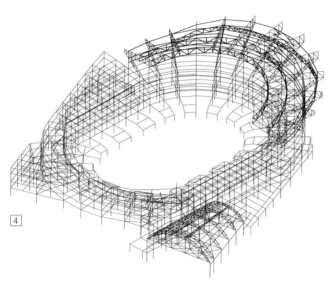

As the upper roof slopes down to the mid-section, support transitions into ten cantilever trusses with backspans that form and support the outer fin walls on the east and west. These tie into the rehearsal hall "horn." Central truss segments dropped into the gap between supports complete the high roof framing (Fig.7). Columns at either side of the stage support trusses that carry the low level of the roof (Figs.8,9).

The engineers sought to simplify the construction process. They analyzed eight construction stages to determine roof loads during various

9 Unlike sports-oriented arenas, this building has a definite "stage end," complete with proscenium framing shown here as bold elements. This framing supports the lowest roof level.

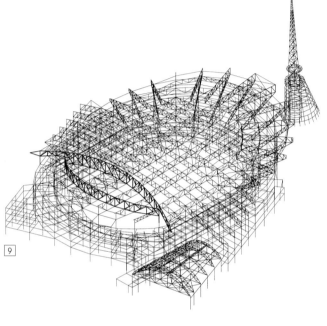

7 For the roof mid-section, side trusses have backup spans that anchor cantilevers to receive the ends of drop in spans. This permitted erection with a minimum of temporary shoring towers. Cranes within the arena bowl begin to place drop-in trusses between midsection cantilevers. Note roof decking is spread as quickly as steel framework is erected.

8 Nearing completion, the design and construction challenges – posed by the three levels of the main roof, the rehearsal hall "horn" and other facilities – are clearly shown.

operations. The process allowed the contractor to minimize supports during construction, and freed up ground level workspace. A two-way truss system supports the mid-level roof. The shorter transverse trusses were placed first. These were mostly self-supporting, with any temporary shoring away from the work areas. Longitudinal trusses were placed afterwards with no shoring (Fig.20). Truss depths varied, with end plates used on the deeper ones to simplify connections. By using standard straight elements and limiting truss depths to a maximum of 14 ft (4.3 m), the engineers eased shipping and minimized hoisting capacity demands (Figs.10-19).

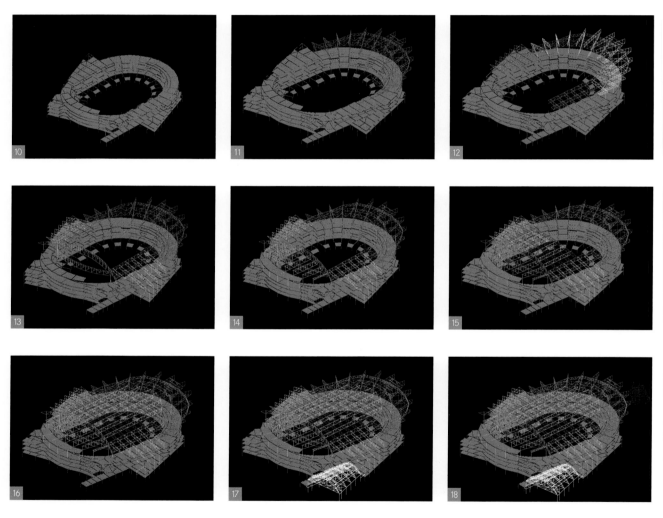

10-19 An erection concept was built into the arena design to permit fast, economical construction. Erection began at the high end with "boomerang" trusses (green) and horseshoe trusses (purple).

Cantilevered mid-section trusses (cyan) and low, heavy proscenium framing (red) followed. Infill trusses (navy blue) and longitudinal secondary trusses (yellow) completed the roof.

A dramatic daylit concourse was tucked under the overhanging seating bowl (Fig.21). It has tall glass walls laterally supported by visually unobtrusive vertical Vierendeel "ladder" trusses (Fig.23). The concourse ceiling features long-span king-post trusses with twinned tension rods to sculpted gusset plates (Fig.22).

After a thermal analysis of the cast-in-place concrete walls, the engineers were able to avoid the need for nearly all the expansion joints one would normally expect, eliminating potential problems and improving esthetics.

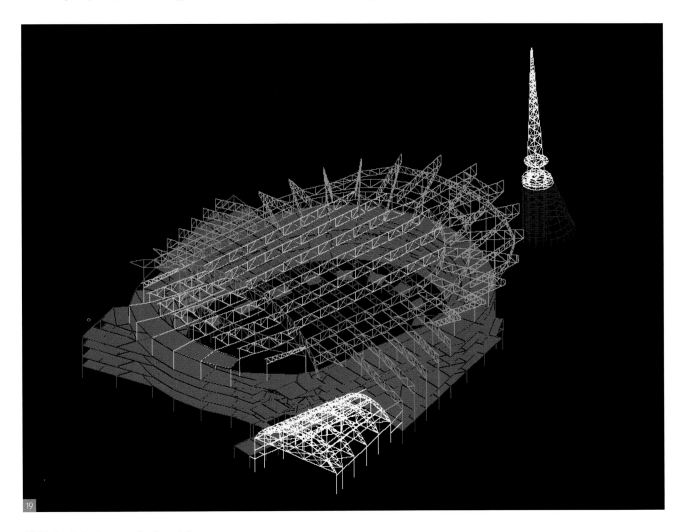

19

20 This longitudinal cross-section through the structural framing shows the step between roof planes at the transition from deep proscenium trusses at left to shallower infill trusses of the midsection and "boomerang" trusses at right.

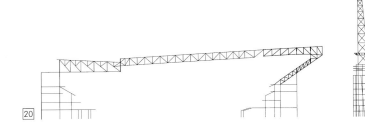

20

The "radio tower" with its elliptical 100 ft (30.5 m) base houses a mini-theater, a sports hall of fame, and an observation deck (Figs.24,25). The 20,000 seat, 1 million square foot (92,903 square meter) Gaylord Entertainment Center opened in 1996.

21 This side of the arena shows the rehearsal hall at left, the glass concourse wall under the roof overhang at right, and mid-section truss backspan fins at center.

22 Visual drama is added to the concourse ceiling by king-post trusses of varying spans with twin steel rod tension ties and sculpted gusset connections.

23 A curving glass wall supported by columns linked to form "ladder" trusses creates a bright, inviting concourse.

Owner
The Sports Authority

Developer
**The Metropolitan Development
and Housing Agency**

Architect
HOK Sport + Venue + Event

Structural Engineer
Thornton-Tomasetti Engineers

Owner's Representative
Turner Construction Co.

General Contractor
Perini Building Co.

Construction Manager
Turner Construction

Other Team Members

Mechanical, Electrical & Plumbing Engineer
Smith Seckman Reid, Inc.
Site/Civil Engineer
Hart Freeland Roberts, Inc.
Geotechnical Consultant
Ogden

24 This view of iconic latticework tower, symbolizing Nashville music broadcasts, is framed by the glazed concourse wall and the overhang of the high seating bowl on "boomerang" trusses

25 The tower tip awaiting erection shows steel plate fins that will glow as a beacon when floodlit at night.

Philips Arena, Atlanta

Asymmetry is the order of the day at the startling Philips Arena in Atlanta, Georgia. The client wanted a high profile structure and the architects, HOK Sport + Venue + Event, Kansas City, Missouri, and Arquitectonica, Miami, Florida, complied. The arena's 200,000 square foot (18,580 square meter) roof is expressed as three overlapping layers that meet at odd angles (Fig.1). Each layer has its own curvature and slope, while all present very thin edges (Fig.4). The design posed some knotty problems for the structural engineers and the contractors.

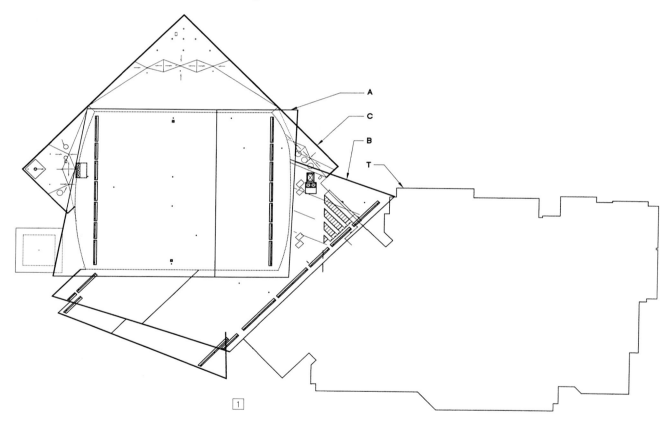

1

1 This complex arena plan with overlapping, skewed roofs shares access with the adjacent tower.
A High roof.
B Intermediate roof level with entry skylights.
C Low roof level.
T CNN office tower.

2 The overlapping, skewed and curved roof surfaces create a "fifth façade" that provides a visual treat to office workers in nearby buildings.

Bernardo Fort-Brescia of Arquitectonica says the curving roof lines were important because they present a "fifth façade" seen from the upper levels of the adjoining CNN building and other skyscrapers (Fig.2). "The arena bowl had a unique asymmetrical shape, and we wanted this asymmetry to be evident in the building's exterior expression. Thornton-Tomasetti Engineers proposed arched trusses that reinforced the roof's formal concept in every respect. The trusses span the bowl following the asymmetry, as well as the vaults that cascade down to the entrance porch" (Fig.3).

The engineers explored variations on the tension tied arch for many long-span structures with unusual geometries. Still, the flamboyant Philips roof was unique. The engineers decided to use twin tied arches along one sideline, accentuating the asymmetry of the seating bowl site (Fig.5).

3 The stepped nature of the roof planes is clear at this "porch," a covered passage supported on exterior columns.

4 Thin, cantilevered roof planes provide architectural drama unusual for a sports facility.

5 Twin tied-arch trusses, 3 ft (0.9 m) apart, leap 275 ft (83.8 m) across the arena space in dramatic fashion, accentuating the unusual asymmetry of the seating bowl and reducing roof spans for economy. Note the wall of stacked suites at lower right.

6 The twinned trusses are 43 ft (13.1 m) deep and were erected in quarters using large prefabricated sections.
A Trussed top chords are less than 13 ft (4 m) deep for easy shipping.
B A W14 x 730 (560 mm deep; 1,090 kg/m) "jumbo column" compression arch carries most of the load.
C W14 x 233 (400 mm deep; 350 kg/m) tension ties resist arch spread, relieving supports.
D W14 (355 mm deep) stubs connecting the trusses provide stability and alternate load paths.
E Steel plates 1 inch (25.4 mm) thick link tension ties for redundancy.

The 275 ft (83.8 m) long arches sit three feet apart at the highest roof level, where they reduced the longer span by 90 ft (27.4 m), and eliminated the need for very long spans in the other direction.

The firm conducted a two-stage analysis of the structural system, one with only the dead load of the steel and one with dead loads for the entire structure plus live loads. The analyses determine the structure's ability to self-support during construction, allowing for minimal shoring and more efficient workspace for the contractors.

The 43 ft (13.1 m) deep arch was erected in quarters from moveable shoring towers, so concrete work could proceed elsewhere in the arena, accelerating progress on the fast-track project. The double tied arches sit on concrete perimeter columns and support the framing for the lower roofs (Fig.6).

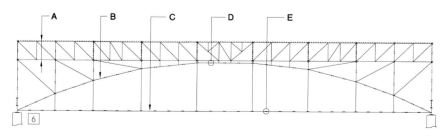

There are two other deep trusses that run along major roof steps; infill purlins and shallow trusses complete the roof support system (Fig.8) and carry an extensive rigging and catwalk system (Fig.7). The structural elements were designed in shippable sizes, no more than 13 ft (4 m) deep, and assembled on site. The twin tied arches and the proscenium arches meet at corner columns with architectural "wedges" that define the different seating areas.

The irregular roof edges use lighter framing, tapering trusses and extended top chords for support (Fig.10). The lowest roof, only about 2 ft (0.6 m) thick, has a grillage of intersecting wide-flange beams (Fig.9). In addition, the thin roof edge is supported along two entrance areas of the arena by structural columns that form the words "CNN" for the company in the adjacent headquarters building, and "ATLANTA" (Fig.13). Architect Fort-Brescia says this idea eliminated the need for major cantilevers.

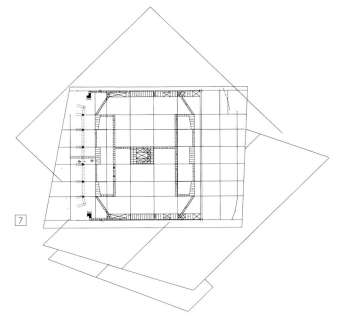

7

7 Extensive catwalks permit rigging and staging a wide variety of events.

8 High roof framing plan.
E Twin truss.
F Line of arena façade below shown dotted.
G Shallow infill truss spanning to twin truss.
H Bridging truss between infill trusses.
P Wide-flange steel purlins between infill trusses.
T1 Roof step truss along transition between high and low roofs.

9 Several levels of lower roofs are shown on this plan. Lowest framing is shown in adjacent part plans.
A Outline of high roof above; dashed lines show grids for main high roof trusses.
B Mid-level roof with longer spans framed by steel joists.
C Lower roof framed with concrete slabs, beams and girders.
D Lower roof framed with long-span steel joists. Arrows lowest part plans have short spans framed with wide-flange beams for shallow construction depths.

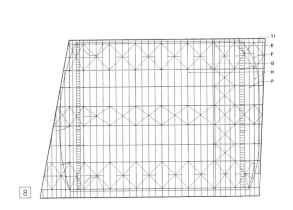

8

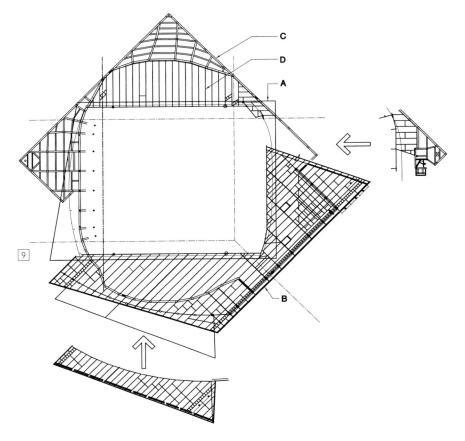

9

At the Philips Arena, all skyboxes, suites and suite services sit on one side of the interior space. The asymmetry in the arena's inner space affords better views for all fans (Fig.11). HOK Sport's Project Manager, Bradd Crowley, says of the complex roof, "the structural support system is prominent from the arena's suites. It had to look good, and Thornton-Tomasetti Engineers are very sensitive to design issues."

The Philips Arena opened in 1999. By collaborating early, the architects and engineers found a structural solution that worked within the esthetic vision while simplifying construction (Fig.12).

10 Roof step trusses, perpendicular to the twin truss, support both high and low roofs. Note twin truss crossing through right support and cantilevering top chord members at each end to create thin roof overhangs.

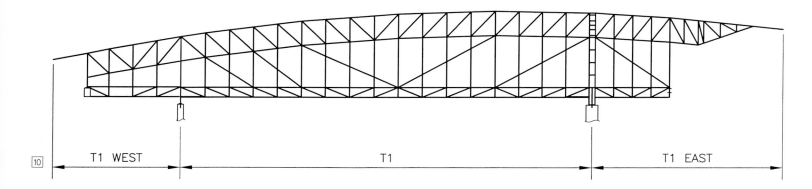

10   T1 WEST   T1   T1 EAST

11 Asymmetrical seating, unusual long-span roof framing and extensive catwalks support entertainment spectaculars in the new Philips Arena.

12 The mix of curved, overlapping roofs, iconic columns and different lighting qualities create a unique, inviting arena.

13 Structural steel columns with architectural cladding spell out the arena's home city of Atlanta while supporting the edge of a low roof.

Owner
Fulton County Recreation Authority

Developer
Turner Sports and Entertainment Development

Architect
HOK Sport + Venue + Event/Arquitectonica

Structural Engineer
Thornton-Tomasetti Engineers

Owner's Representative
Janet Marie Smith/Barton Malow

General Contractor
Beers Construction Company

Other Team Members

Local Structural Engineer
Cecil Chan (Foundations)
Mechanical, Electrical & Plumbing Engineer
ME Engineers
Steel Subcontractor
Qualico Steel

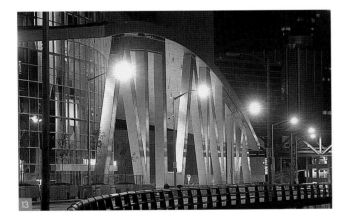

Pepsi Center, Denver

The owners of the Pepsi Center in Denver, Colorado, had a daunting list of demands for the designers and contractors, including a strict 21-month schedule for completion of the 675,000 square foot (62,709 square meter) arena, and a firm $90 million budget. The project team met those requirements with a sophisticated arena roof solution that used only 17 pounds of structural steel per square foot (83 kg per square meter). There were larger planning and design issues as well: the project, sited on an abandoned railroad yard, was part of a major urban revitalization effort. HOK Sport + Venue + Event, Kansas City, Missouri, had to create a "context where there was none," says Chris Carver, the Project Architect for the center (Fig.1). The goal was an amenity that would attract people, tie the arena to downtown, and encourage future development.

1 Sited on an old railroad yard, Pepsi Center created its own architectural context and incorporated a structurally efficient long-span roof.

2 A "racetrack" plan was used to structural advantage, mixing semi-circular ends with tied arches across the central flat zone.
Legend for three plans and truss section:
A Main roof truss top chords span 350 ft (106.7 m) across the arena width.
B Bridging trusses keep trusses stable during and after erection.
C Radial trusses span from perimeter columns to the central hub.
D Roof purlins are a mix of W10 and W14 sizes (254 mm and 356 mm deep) to support curved roofing on segmented truss chords.
E Roof plane bracing stabilizes trusses.
H Trussed central hub or spine.
P Inverted pyramid forms a king-post between hub and tension tie.
R Ring truss provides resistance to hoop forces and permits load redistribution.
T Steel wide-flange tension tie (in a different plane).

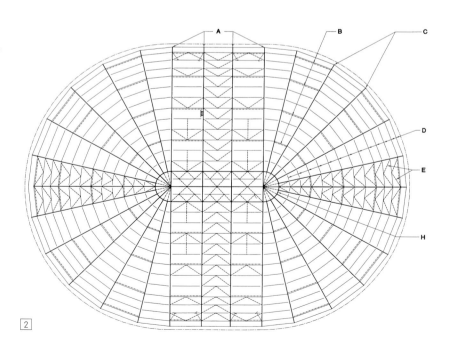

Arena roofs usually drive a project because of their cost. HOK Sport worked closely with Thornton-Tomasetti Engineers to find the optimum roof design. Their collaboration resulted in an ingenious roof that fulfills load-bearing and sight line requirements and presents an airy yet dramatic esthetic in a constructible and economical system.

The design is a variation on the trussed-chord tied arch arena roof concept that Thornton-Tomasetti Engineers has refined over the years. All shop-fabricated components are sufficiently shallow for easy shipping by highway, and the system is very light compared to truss systems like old-fashioned railroad bridges with full-depth diagonals.

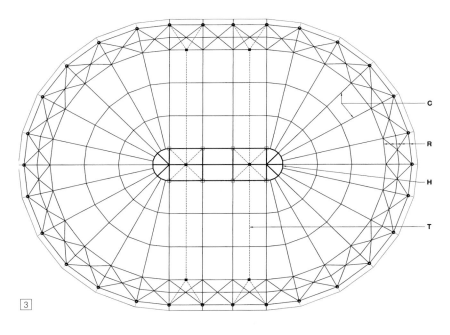

3 Plan view of the lower-level edge of top chord trusses shows radial trusses stopping at the central hub, and tension ties below as dashed lines.

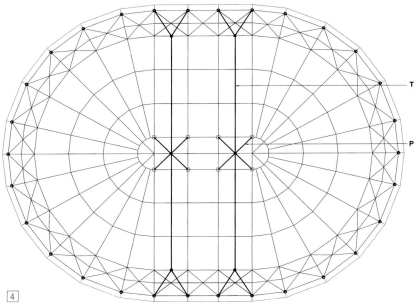

4 Tension ties, pyramid posts and end "Y" details are shown bold in this lowest-level plan. Four trusses share two tension ties for construction efficiency, improved sight lines and structural drama.

The oval roof, 450 ft (137.2 m) by 350 ft (106.7 m) in plan, offered a challenge and an opportunity. The engineers treated the racetrack shape as a dome split down the middle, separated by flat-sided inserts (Fig.2). This design concept incorporated the inherent efficiency of the dome without the dome's requirement for a tension ring around its base. For this geometry, the flat sides of the roof must work as an arch. A central boxed spine is carried by four trussed-chord tied arches spanning straight across the arena's 350 ft (106.7 m) width (Fig.5). The arches work in pairs, with each pair sharing a tension tie through an inverted four-strut pyramidal king post that creates an effective truss depth of 50 ft (15.2 m) (Fig.3,4).

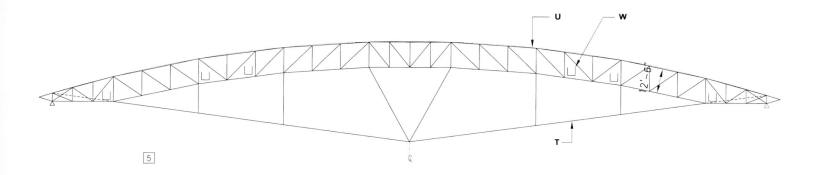

5

5 Main trusses spanning 350 ft (106.7 m) across the arena are actually tied arches.
U Upper chord truss is an arch shallow enough to ship in pre-assembled segments.
W Walkways and catwalks are integrated with the trusses.

6 The tension tie is split at this "Y" detail to engage two roof truss top chords. The bolted connections are quite compact considering the large forces carried.

By reducing the number of tension tie locations, this design minimized steel, simplified construction and improved sight lines. The ties included twin wide-flange steel members for reasonable connection details and improved redundancy (Fig.6,7). The inverted king-post trusses also added structural drama (Fig.8).

The rounded sections of the oval roof are "half domes" comprised of radial trussed ribs that span from the central box spine to the roof perimeter (Fig.9). The roof system design cut the length of the radial trusses to 155 ft (47.2 m), with depths of only 12.5 ft (3.8 m). These trusses could be shipped to the site and erected in one piece, saving time. The system can accommodate loads of up to 90 tons (81 metric tons) for scoreboards and other rigging.

7 Twin wide-flange members form the tension ties connection to pyramidal king posts under the central hub. Using two members permits smaller, more practical connections and offers improved redundancy of load paths.

8 The bold arrangement of ties and pyramids is clear in this construction photograph.

The design necessitated shoring towers for erection, but their costs were offset by other efficiencies. The four transverse arches and two inverted king-post pyramids rested on eight shoring towers clustered at center court (Fig.10). The larger structural components were shop-assembled, shipped to the site in 155 ft (47.2 m) lengths and directly lifted into place (Fig.11). This allowed simultaneous work in other areas below, such as installation of the precast concrete seating bowl (Figs.12,13). The system required minimal field splicing, and the repetitive construction saved time and helped meet the tight deadlines.

9 Radial trusses span from central hub to perimeter concrete posts and moment frames built into the concrete concourses. No radial tension ties are needed, simplifying construction and roof appearance.

Two striking glass atria are the entries to the Pepsi Center. Both are 75 ft (22.9 m) high, designed to "draw people in, to activate street level activity," says Carver (Fig.16). The glass expanse is structurally supported by 30 inch (762 mm) steel-encased perimeter columns that are part of the architectural statement (Figs.14,15).

10 The central hub or spine was assembled atop eight tall shoring towers at center court, leaving the seating bowl unencumbered and allowing for early installation of precast seating units.

11 Trusses spanning from perimeter to hub were placed in one piece, speeding erection. Here the "Y"-link to the tension tie is clearly visible.

The arena's cast-in-place concrete floor slab was designed with shrinkage strips, temporary gaps in construction, instead of expansion joints. Thornton-Tomasetti worked with the contractor to reduce and locate the strips for minimal schedule impact. Carver says using the strips enhanced the arena's esthetics: "expansion joints are messy, difficult to maintain and do not work well with high-end floor materials."

The Pepsi Center seats 20,000 and has 95 luxury suites, a 300-seat restaurant and a column-free practice court 70 by 130 ft (21.3 by 39.6 m) in plan. The arena opened in 1999, on time and within budget.

12 White shoring towers under the hub are visible in this construction photo. Note roof decking was spread quickly as steel trusses were placed.

13 In this image, the seating bowl is progressing below as trusses are placed above, shaving important months off the construction schedule.

14 Reflective glass transforms the atria into dramatic abstract objects by day.

15 The atria provide a welcoming glow at night.

16 Two tall glazed atria signal inviting entry points to the arena.

Owner
Ascent Entertainment Group

Architect
HOK Sport + Venue + Event

Structural Engineer
Thornton-Tomasetti Engineer

General Contractor
M. A. Mortenson

Construction Manager
M. A. Mortenson

Other Team Members

Mechanical, Electrical & Plumbing
ME Engineers
Soils Consultant
CTL/Thompson
Steel Fabricator
W & W Steel Company
Steel Erector
Derr Construction

Soldier Field, Chicago

Chicago's Soldier Field was built in the late 1920's as a sports stadium dedicated to commemorating the American soldiers who died in World War I. The memorial has colonnades with neoclassical columns and is one of the city's many prized landmarks. The stadium, however, was no longer competitive with newer sports facilities and was in need of major structural repairs. Team owners wanted skyboxes and other amenities, but updating the arena became a cause célèbre in the architecturally attuned city. The historic colonnades could not be altered, but a typical football seating bowl, if fit between them, would have made the playing field 150 ft (45.7 m) too narrow (Fig.1). Since a football field is 160 ft (49 m) wide, that clearly would have been impractical.

This dilemma had an ingenious architectural solution. The Boston firm of Wood + Zapata, working with Lohan Caprile Goettsch of Chicago, set a modern stadium within and above the existing building shell (Figs.3,6,16). A new steel-clad, steel-framed structure to the west sits on new foundations and flares out above existing concrete walls and iconic colonnades, which visitors can walk through for the first time in decades (Figs.2,15). The

1 The historic colonnades along each side of old Soldier Field could not be touched or altered in the new stadium design.

2 The west grandstand was intentionally designed as a sleek modern object to maintain a clear demarcation between the new stadium and historic elements of the war memorial.

3 The Soldier Field project is part of a larger renovation of Chicago's treasured lakefront parks.

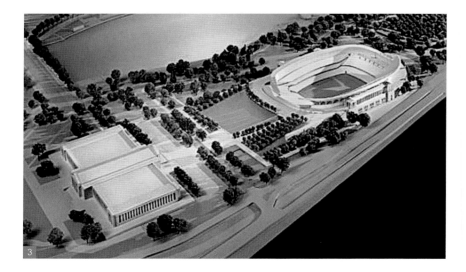

asymmetrical seating pattern offers improved sight lines, and ample preferential seating areas (club seats and skyboxes) make the stadium business economics work. The renovated stadium will be the centerpiece of a 17-acre lakefront area recreational upgrade that includes underground parking.

Soldier Field's owner, the Chicago Park District, leases the stadium to the Chicago Bears football team. Alice Hoffman was Project Manager for the Chicago Bears. She says it was imperative that the new stadium would not be supported by the old one, or in any way interfere with the historic structure. Hoffman adds that Thornton-Tomasetti and the architects joined the design team at the same time and their collaboration began immediately. The result is a final design that maintains the visual and physical integrity of the colonnades (Figs.8,9). Thornton-Tomasetti Engineers faced several unusual tasks on this prestigious project. One was the upper grandstand seating area, from which fans will have a view of nearby Lake Michigan. Inward-reaching cantilevers are a common seating feature (Fig.4). To clear over the colonnade, seats also rest on long cantilevers extending away from the field, a unique condition. Small, repetitive forces, as from fans' stamping feet, can cause building motions that are safe but annoying. After thorough analysis, the engineers concluded that a series of tuned mass dampers along the outer edge of the cantilevered area was necessary for audience comfort (Fig.5).

4 Seating bowl features cantilevers towards the field to bring fans close to the game. Note cantilevered framing for video displays at the far end of the field.

5 Curving steel plate girder rakers cantilever far above supporting struts, so concrete slabs set on edge, visible behind the top trusses, are used for tuned mass dampers that control vibration. Note Sears Tower visible beyond the memorial colonnade.

6 Each end of the main grandstand is dramatically sliced at an angle, revealing slender support struts beyond.

7 Video display scoreboards extending horizontally 100 feet rely on this cantilevered trusswork for support.

Concealed within the rear parapet wall are a series of 20 ton (18 metric ton) slabs of concrete-filled steel boxes ("mass") standing edgewise on spring supports. Tuned to bounce out of phase with the cantilevered seating, they push and pull on dampers (shock absorbers) mounted between seating and slabs. By converting the kinetic energy of motion into heat energy, the dampers reduce vibration amplitude. This is probably the first use of such dampers in a U.S. stadium. Another cantilever challenge was the support of two high-tech video boards at either end of the structure. These boards jut out almost 100 ft (30 m) beyond the upper stadium framing to provide spectators with larger-than-life views of the games (Figs.7,10). Opposite the grandstand are glassed-in skyboxes, where the glazing is tilted towards the field to enhance viewing angles (Figs.11,13,14). Some of the lowest level seats are removable for other sports or entertainment events. The new steel structure sits on precast concrete pile caps, and the loads it imposes required 2,000 H-piles 95 ft (29 m) long.

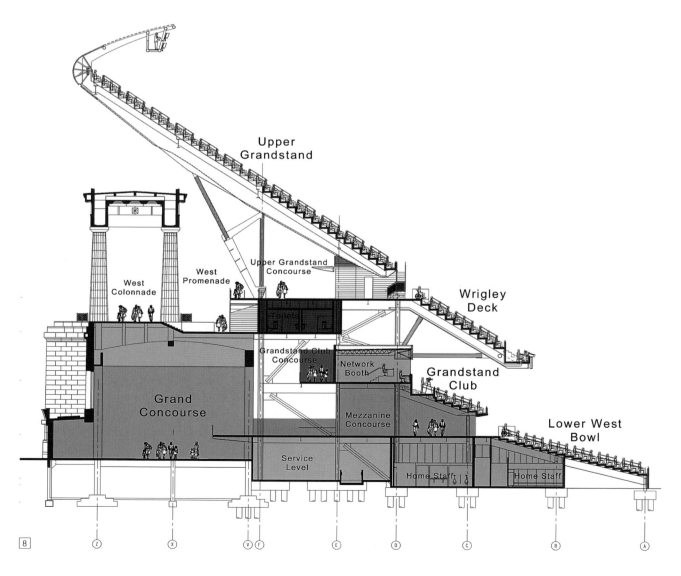

Thornton-Tomasetti used Xsteel, a 3-D computer modeling tool typically used by European designers and fabricators, to accurately describe the complex geometry of the stadium framing. Xsteel allowed the designers, steel fabricators, and the contractors to use the system simultaneously. This was a great advantage considering the severe constraints imposed by the old structure. Usually projects have analysts, designers, detailers and fabricators working in separate systems. Structural analysis may be performed using 3-D computer models as "wire frames" with beams and columns shown as dimensionless center lines. Designers develop contract documents showing member sizes and orientations on 2-D sheets for particular plan, section and elevation viewpoints. Detailers then create their own, more explicit and elaborate shop drawings for each piece of steel. Finally, marks are placed on the steel to guide the fabrication workers.

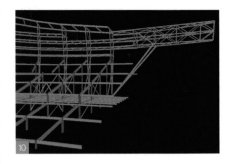

8,9 This cross-section through mid-field shows the left grandstands extending over an historic colonnade, and right skyboxes with inward-leaning walls for game visibility.

10 The Xsteel computer program precisely represented every piece of the structural frame for coordination among designers, fabricators and erectors. This view shows south scoreboard framing.

11 A swooping extension of the skybox structure terminates in the north scoreboard cantilever.

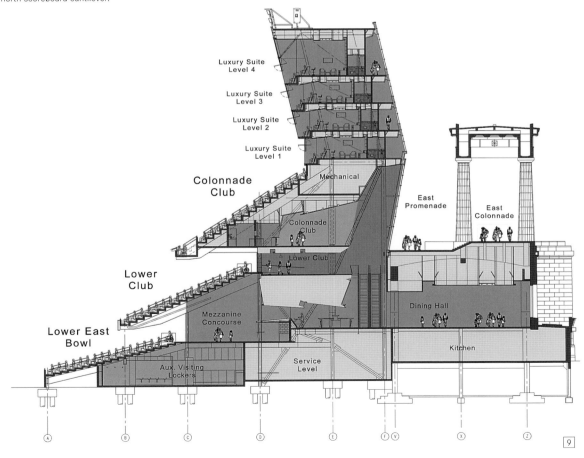

In contrast, Xsteel is designed as a system that all parties can use to great benefit. Although starting as a "wire frame" model, the frame provided a true representation of the physical conditions. Designers can see in 3-D how the structural steel and connections fit together. Detailers add more specific information (i.e., bolt sizes, locations) while checking that connections are practical to assemble based on surrounding members (Fig.12). The detailed model information is used to drive CNC (Computer Numeric Controlled) fabrication machines that cut and drill steel precisely. By building more information into one model, rather than having separate systems, Xsteel avoided potential field problems and accelerated erection. Soldier Field was a fast-track project, and met the mandated deadline of the fall 2003 football season's opening day.

12 The Xsteel computer program represented structural framing so accurately that detailed steel fabrication was based on it, down to the smallest joints.

13 This dramatic view of the pipe struts under the cantilevered scoreboard shows the seating bowl at right and Lake Michigan and the old colonnade in the background at left.

14 Complex curves and slopes at these skyboxes would have been much more difficult to complete without the use of the Xsteel program as a design, detailing and coordination tool.

Owner
Chicago Park District

Developer
The Chicago Bears

Architect
**LW+Z, a Joint Venture of Lohan Caprile
Goettsch Architects and Wood + Zapata**

Structural Engineer
Thornton-Tomasetti Engineers

General Contractor
**TBMK, A Joint Venture of Turner Construction
Co., Barton Malow Co. and Kenny
Construction**

Project Manager
Hoffman Management Partners LLC.

Other Team Members

Local Structural Engineer
Soodan & Associates
Mechanical, Electrical Engineer
Ellerbe Becket
Site/Civil Engineer
V3 Consultants
Geotechnical Engineer
STS Consultants
Sports Design Consultants
Ellerbe Becket
Landscape Architects
**Peter Lindsay Schaudt
Landscape Architects, Inc.**

15 The steel of the new portion of Soldier Field contrasts sharply with the restored colonnade at right.

16 Seen from a distance, the dramatic arc of the addition is silhouetted against the sky.

Ford Field, Detroit

Project size and scale are important design and construction considerations. In Detroit, Michigan, Ford Field is a new, fully enclosed, multi-use stadium that successfully addresses these issues. This home of the Detroit Lions can seat over 65,000 football fans under a vast roof that stretches 770 ft by 640 ft (234.7 m by 195.1 m) and stands 200 ft (61 m) high (Fig.1). The roof expanse includes two 90 ft (27.4 m) cantilevers over a renovated department store warehouse, now part of the stadium complex (Fig.2). The adaptive re-use of the warehouse was a result of negotiations with the city government.

1 65,000 football fans watch the Detroit Lions play under a high roof spanning 770 ft by 640 ft (234.7 m by 195.1 m). Translucent panels backlight the massive trusses.

2 Along this wall, an historic warehouse building was renovated and incorporated within the new stadium complex. Roof supports were threaded through the existing building.

In spite of these outsize dimensions, there are no columns within the viewing area, a requirement by the owners, William Clay Ford, Senior and Junior, of the Ford Motor Company. As a result, there is not a bad seat in the house, says Project Executive Architect Michael McGunn of the Detroit-based SmithGroup. The final high roof system incorporates only eight columns and four main trusses, all outside and above the viewing area. Referring to the roof as the stadium's crowning achievement, the architect credits Thornton-Tomasetti Engineers for making the massive roof system "seem easy."

Lateral roof loads posed a challenge, as they could not be resisted by the historic warehouse incorporated into the building's south side. Instead, the loads are delivered from the roof to foundations just clear of the warehouse by two cast-in-place concrete supercolumns, each 18 ft (5.5 m) in diameter and 105 ft (32 m) tall (Fig.3). Their foundations are also substantial, square

3 Roof lateral stability is provided by concrete supercolumns under the steel roof trusses. This avoided adverse effects on the historic warehouse being renovated at right.

4 Supercolumn gravity and lateral loads are resisted by caisson-supported concrete pile caps 27 ft square (8.2 m), like the one about to be cast in this excavation. The worker shows the scale of construction.

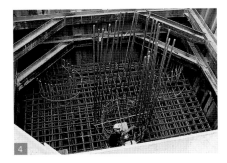

175

pile caps 27 ft (8.2 m) on each side and 8 ft (2.4 m) deep, supported on five caissons extending as far as 125 ft (38.1 m) down to bedrock (Fig.4). Two more concrete columns, in plan each a square, 6 ft (1.8 m) on a side, sit between the supercolumns. One is threaded through the warehouse, and the other is located in an alleyway next to it. Along the north side of the stadium, four concrete columns 5 ft square (1.5 m) rise from the concrete-framed concourse structure (Fig.5). These shorter columns share the roof loads and contribute to roof lateral stability through frame action. Four long-span trusses cross the playing field and seating bowl, with one end of each truss sitting on one of the eight columns. The two outside trusses span 550 ft (167.6 m) across the field, bear on supercolumns, and then cantilever an additional 90 ft (27.4 m) over the warehouse. These trusses have arched top chords supporting high roof framing and level bottom chords that support adjacent low roofs. The two interior trusses span 640 ft (195.1 m) and have sloping bottom chords to provide field clearance (Fig.6).

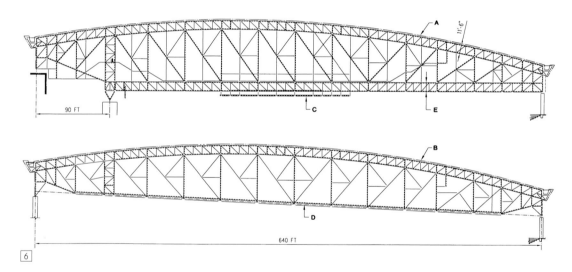

5 Concourse floors of Ford Field are cast-in-place concrete, with sloping rakers supporting precast concrete stadia, or seating units.

6 Two types of steel trusses carry the high roof. Each has twin planes of truss diagonals. Trussed chords were shallow enough to shop-fabricate and ship assembled, speeding construction.
A Box trussed top chord for side trusses;
  the cantilevered left end clears over an historic renovated warehouse building
  (shown by heavy lines).
B Box trussed top chord for middle trusses.
C Suspended framing for scoreboard support.
D Four-member sloping bottom chords for seating sight lines and clearances.
E Box trussed bottom chord for side trusses to receive adjacent low roofs.

At the highest point of the curved roof, the main trusses are over 90 ft (27.4 m) deep. Six lines of bridging trusses run between the long-span trusses, providing a horizontally stiff diaphragm without requiring complex horizontal bracing or counting on roof decking (Fig.7).

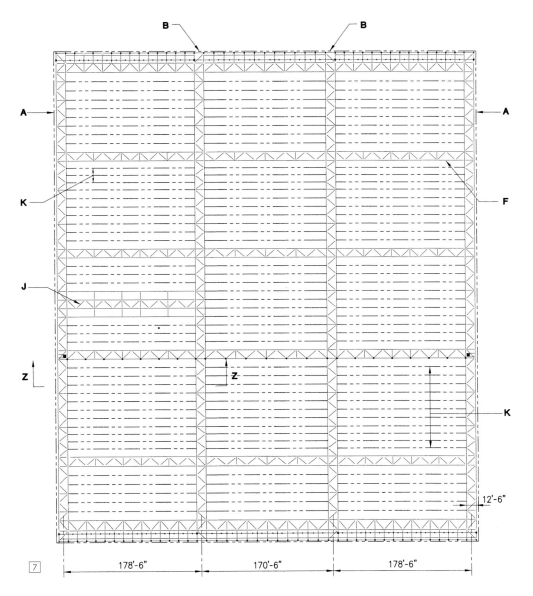

7 High roof boxed main span chords and bridging trusses form a diaphragm for lateral loads. This permits use of simple, economical drop-in roof joists and light metal decking, and avoids complex bracing systems.

A Roof step adjacent to side truss top chords.
B Middle truss top chords.
F Bridging trusses link main trusses.
J Additional trusses for Jumbotron graphical display support.
K Infill joists spanning between main trusses; spacing varies to carry snow drift loads using the same roof deck and joist sizes.
Z Section through step from high to low roof.

Truss lines also extend across the lower roofs to support heavy concrete-filled roof slabs, mechanical equipment and snow drifts (Fig.8). Steel open-web joists span between main trusses to economically support the upper roof deck. Economies came from optimal material usage, efficient shop fabrication systems and repetition: joists were re-spaced, rather than re-sized, in locations of higher predicted wind and snow loads. Each main and bridging truss has boxed top and bottom chords. Compared to single members, boxed chords have improved redundancy and better erection stability. The top chords have four parallel wide-flange corner members linked by diagonal bracing in vertical and horizontal planes. The box dimensions, 11.5 ft (3.5 m) deep and 12.5 ft (3.8 m) wide, permitted complete assembly of chord segments in the shop, simplifying field work.

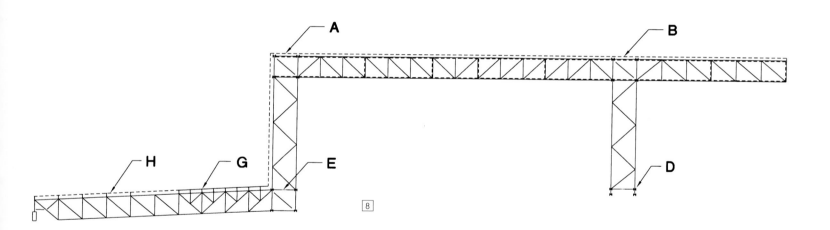

8 Section ZZ, as cut in Fig.7; the main arena roof steps down over seating areas.
A Four-member boxed top chord for side truss shown in cross-section.
B Four-member boxed top chord for middle truss.
D Bottom chord of four parallel wide-flange steel members.
E Boxed bottom chord along low roof.
G Low roof truss has additional members and local concrete slab for rooftop mechanical equipment and snow-drift loads.
H Low roof with metal roof deck.

The top and bottom chords were joined on site with vertical and diagonal members every 45.5 ft (13.9 m) on center. Truss assembly was performed on the ground, with pairs of trusses and infill framing completed as a unit (Fig.9). The units were then lifted to their final elevation by hydraulic strand jacks. This innovative approach avoided the cost and complications of conventional piecewise erection at final elevation on numerous temporary shoring towers. Ground assembly and jacking improved site safety and allowed construction to proceed simultaneously in other areas of the stadium. The structural engineers and the contractor coordinated the installation, which included two lifts of 5.4 million pounds (2,450 metric tons) each. Over 200 tons (180 metric tons) of equipment, including scoreboards and lighting, hang from the long-span trusses. The stadium and the warehouse together enclose 1.3 million square feet (120,773 square meters) of space.

9 Pairs of main trusses were assembled on the ground, along with connecting trusses and roof framing, for speed and safety. The assemblies were then jacked to final elevation.

Ford Field has a glass entryway, a 90 ft (27.4 m) high glass curtain wall that curves for 210 ft (64 m) and looks out on downtown Detroit (Fig.12). The architectural concept called for minimal interference with the views, so the engineers designed steel pipe Vierendeel trusses to support the glass without the clutter of diagonal members (Fig.10). Translucent wall panels cover the step between the high and low roofs; when the stadium is lit up at night, the pattern of the long-span structural system is dramatically visible. The glass curtain wall and the translucent panels are graceful notes for this monumental stadium (Fig.11). Ford Field opened in July 2002 at a total cost of $500 million.

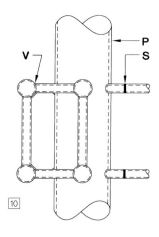

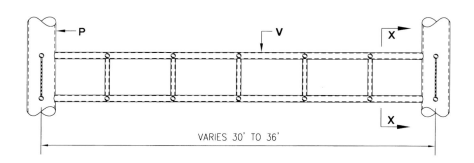

VARIES 30' TO 36'

10 A Vierendeel truss system without diagonals minimizes visual obstructions behind the glazed entry wall. The left image is Section XX as cut at right.

P Glazed wall main columns of steel pipe 24 inches (610 mm) in diameter, carry roof load and lateral wind load in a two-way grid of Vierendeel trusses.

S Vierendeel pipe chords between main columns were field-spliced with full-penetration welds.

V Vierendeel box trusses of 4.5 inch (114 mm) and 8.75 inch (222 mm) diameter steel pipe span horizontally between main columns and follow the gentle curve of the glazed wall.

11 The completed Ford Field features a high, arched roof stepping down to a curved wall at the main entry.

Owner
Detroit/Wayne County Stadium Authority

Architect
SmithGroup/Rossetti Associates

Structural Engineer
Thornton-Tomasetti Engineers

General Contractor
Hunt Construction Group Inc.

Owner's Representative/Project Manager
Hammes Company

Other Team Members

Mechanical, Electrical & Plumbing Engineer
SmithGroup
Geotechnical Engineer
Somat Engineering
Steel Fabricator & Detailer
ADF
Steel Erector
SCI/Steelcon
Erectors' Engineer
Ruby & Associates P.C.
Lift Erector
John Gibson Projects, Ltd.

12 A 90 ft (27.4 m) high glazed wall creates an
inviting main entry and provides fans with a view of
Detroit.

Acknowledgments

This book could not have been completed without
the contributions of Leonard M. Joseph, Principal
of The Thornton-Tomasetti Group, whose combination
of engineering expertise and language skills is rare
indeed. His critiques were always on the mark and
his patience and attention to detail invaluable.
The firm's Co-Chairmen, Richard L. Tomasetti and
Dr. Charles H. Thornton were wonderfully supportive,
as were the Managing Principals and the engineering
staff. I spent countless hours interviewing and
re-interviewing engineers about the firm's philosophy
and the technical details of the many structures
included in the book. Without exception, everyone
displayed unfailing courtesy, high enthusiasm and
willingness to help with this book. That attitude says
a great deal about the firm's culture. I am also grateful
for the insights provided by Thornton-Tomasetti's
collaborators, the architects, developers and contractors who worked with them on these projects.
Finally, I owe thanks to many members of Thornton-
Tomasetti's staff, notably Mary Findlen, Bethany
Carlson, Doris Cheng, Vanessa Liguori, Suzanne
Clemmer and Carol Moy, who helped immensely in
organizing and coordinating the material for this
book. My thanks also go to Ria Stein, the editor who
initiated this book, for her patience and encourage-
ment, and to Sabine Bennecke whose enthusiasm
and attention to detail was much appreciated.
It was my pleasure to work with such dedicated
professionals.

Virginia Fairweather

Credits